Introduction

The face of the VC10. The main windscreen panels/frame were Vickers Vanguard toolings. RAF VC10 seen close up.

INTRODUCTION
VC10: Powerful Symbol of British Jetliner Prowess

There are many famous civil aircraft that are icons of their type or era. The Caravelle, the Concorde, the Boeing 747 and the 707, the DC-8 – to name just a few of civil aviation's defining airframes. Amongst them ranks the Vickers VC10 – also known as the British Aircraft Corporation VC10, and as the larger, more powerful Super VC10. The VC10 was the final fanfare from a golden age of British aviation and despite the fact that it lost its commercial battle with the Boeing 707, it retains a place in the hearts and minds of aviation fans all over the world.

Inside the Vickers family of aircraft, from Viscount to Valiant to 'Vanjet' studies and to VC10 first-flight, this VC10 tale is a great story of design triumph, despite fluctuating corporate and political events.

The VC10 marked a new beginning to the second generation of jetliner design; it also marked the end of British design and manufacture of large civil airlines, Concorde excepted. Indeed, Concorde was (in British terms) designed and engineered by the men who had created the VC10. Former VC10 engineers and designers also worked at Boeing and influenced several aspects of the 747's systems design.

Few airliners have engendered the love and loyalty that the VC10 did across its crews and passengers and it was not just its dramatic aerodynamically sculpted looks that made it a favourite. VC10 flew and handled like a fighter, being overpowered and overequipped with lift. Here was the first full application of four rear-mounted engines, a safe T-tail design, an advanced high-lift wing and multiple fail-safe systems amid an overengineered airframe of massive strength.

The VC10 was designed to meet the exacting demands of the airline that ordered it – the British Overseas Airways Corporation (BOAC), the pre-1974 antecedent of today's British Airways (which began operations under such name at that time).

"In the VC10 BOAC got what they asked for." So said (the late) Brian Trubshaw, the famous Concorde and VC10 test pilot with whom the author worked to record the VC10's story.

Sadly, BOAC went on to criticize the VC10. This impacted it sales success on the world's stage. It would be years before the truth came out and by then it was too late.

As planned from the start, the Royal Air Force (RAF) also operated its own specific VC10 variants and made a huge success of them in transport uplift – then latterly as air refuelling tankers.

In engineering and design terms, to meet its specification, VC10 was in one sense advanced. But in another, it was overengineered, overpowered and a touch overweight. These factors have been used to detract from the aircraft's reputation by

The captain's instruments and main controls of A40-AB. The VC10 innovated new ergonomic controls. Note the blue Vickers-Armstrong control column badge.

those who favour the earlier airliners that were the Boeing 707 and the Douglas DC-8. But the facts are that the VC10 was never designed to mimic such competitors and should not be criticized for not doing what it was not designed to do.

The 707 and DC-8 were straightforward machines with cost appeal on normal airline routes from normal, average runways in normal airline use. VC10 was designed to do something very different in a very specific, very British application that was wrapped up in the circumstances of the legacy of the British Empire, its airways, and its tropical operating conditions.

The VC10, and its closest competitor, the 707, were designed for different tasks at different times. The VC10 was an expensive engineering solution to a unique specification, but the fact remains that it did offer aspects of design and application that were more advanced than the 707. The Douglas DC-8 would prove to be sleeker and faster than the 707, but no match for the VC10 in airfield performance.

Was the intercontinental Boeing 707 variant really so much cheaper to run? What of the VC10's combined payload and range advantages, as opposed to the developed 707's longer range but lower maximum payload-range abilities? What of the VC10's ability to uplift and perform in extreme operating circumstances whilst 707s and DC-8s struggled? What of the VC10's requirement for less maintenance, fewer repairs and longer airframe life?

The VC10 used dramatically less runway to take off than any competitor and climbed away more safely. Its slower landing speed addressed very real safety concerns over ever-higher jet airliner landing speeds, notably that of the 707.

A VC10 could lift off with a full load from a short, high-altitude tropical runway in hot, 35°-plus temperatures, in many thousands of feet less runway distance than a 707 or DC-8, and then climb at a nearly 20-degree angle and continue without refuelling to a long-haul destination. No competitor could match this. True, a VC10 could not lift nearly 200 passengers from London Heathrow to Los Angeles in one go, but neither could an early 707, and while a later 707 could do this, that machine could not offer a VC10's payload-range performance in more demanding conditions. The enlarged Super VC10 attempted to match the 707-300/-400 series by trading runway performance for range and more seats but was itself constrained by BOAC's demands.

The VC10 was also emeshed in the process of the British state, of the government's running of, and interference in BOAC as the national airline. BOAC was beholden to the government that funded it and the edicts of a revolving door of politicians, civil servants, and appointed chairmen and boards of directors.

From such circumstances came an airliner and an RAF transport machine that carved a massive mark upon the world and which headlined great British design and technology. Sir George Edwards and his team at Vickers ensured that the VC10 advanced the art of airliner engineering and ability.

One thing is for sure: VC10 opened up the routes and airports of Africa and Asia prior to the great boom in air travel and the advent of the Boeing 747.

Machined from solid, reinforced materials and, stiffer, safer and with low aerodynamic drag from its advanced wings and smooth body, VC10 was faster in the cruise yet a vital 20 knots slower than its competitors when it needed to be – on final approach to landing – thus enhancing safety. A VC10 still holds the record for the fastest commercial airliner crossing of the North Atlantic – at just under two minutes over five hours. Quick to take off, slow to land, able to use much shorter runways and a superbly stable air-to-air refuelling tanker, VC10 brought many benefits.

The swept-finned, Rolls-Royce-powered VC10 flew in service across five decades from 1964, nearly into 2014, and remains a stunning machine adored by many. African airlines loved the VC10. Pan Am came so close to ordering it, but perhaps was never going to be allowed to do that.

Despite its 50-year history, the fact was that however superb in every respect, the VC10 project, did through no fault of its own, signal the end of British large civil airframe design and manufacture.

The loss of the potential VC10 derivatives that were all ready to go from the Vickers/BAC drawing boards – from the true 200+-seater Super VC10 proposals, cargo and combi machines, and the idea of an RB-211-engined conversion – all frame a great waste.

"The VC10 had to be better than the 707, not just different and we succeeded that requirement in many ways." So said Sir George Edwards OM, CBE, FRS, FRAeS – the VC10's instigator and leader prior to creating Concorde.

The VC10 project and its 54 production airframes was a unique, quality-design product born into an age where accountants and corporate men did not want exquisite solutions but rather an effective common denominator. VC10's fate was to be a thoroughbred solution to a problem that only briefly existed: tropical runways which were soon lengthened to accommodate the 707 and the DC-8. We should also recall the VC10's excellent safety record in the context of the accident-strewn airline era in which it flew.

The Russian Il-62 was the world's only other rear-engined, T-tail four-jet airliner. Touted as a VC10 rival or copy, it suffered major aerodynamic stability problems and encountered several fatal crashes as result, this also from its inability to contain an engine failure in the rear-mounted engine pods.

VC10 is also a modellers' favourite and an enduring aviation enthusiasts' subject of affection and interest.

Despite making its last flight on 25 September 2013, the VC10 still has active airframes that are taxied and displayed at events. These are the RAF's ex-ZA147, and ZA241. ZA150 remains 'live' as an

The very clean design and smooth aerodynamic finish can be seen in this fine head-on study of an RAF VC10. Note T-tail and its bullet fairing.

airframe. Numerous VC10 airframes, cockpits and fuselage sections abound – notably at St Athan South Wales Aviation Museum, Brooklands Museum, Cosford, Bruntingthorpe, Duxford, Dunsfold, East Midlands Aero Park, Avro Heritage Museum, Cornwall Aviation Heritage Centre, and of note in Gulf Air livery at Sharjah where ex-East African Airways 5X-UVJ, lastly registered as RAF VC10 K3.ZA149, now resides at the Al Mahatta Museum.

Bringing the VC10 story up to date, this book is a new, concise yet detailed history of the design, development and use of the VC10 amid the affection that endures towards it.

101 Squadron 85th Anniversary markings seen on the tail of XV80, the RAF VC1-C.Mk.1 delivered in July 1966 and latterly converted to C.Mk.1K.

Design & Development

Vickers V1000 rendering depicts its advanced design of 1955. Note the early use of curved tailfin shape.

In 1946, British post-war aircraft development raced ahead in both its military and civil themes. The pro-turbine powered Vickers Viscount dominated the world stage, yet the Bristol Brabazon sank without trace. However, de Havilland's Comet pioneered the concept of the intercontinental *jet* airliner – or 'jetliner'. But its fatal structural problems and consequent grounding set British airline advancement backwards and the subsequent Comet 4 remained a smaller, sub-100 seat jetliner designed for rich people, not mass transport.

While the British airlines dithered with decisions about prop power or jet power, and went off on the prop-turbine side track of the Bristol Britannia and Vickers Vanguard, America, notably Boeing, and subsequently, Douglas, framed their own large, four-jet engined airliner requirements. Britain's BOAC spent several years exploring and planning for a jet-propelled future, only to end such expensively developed plans and enter a brief diversion into a prop future with the Bristol Britannia, then to suddenly seize upon the jet-powered Boeing 707.

In the British industry lay ideas for the Bristol 200 and a Handley Page jet airliner based upon the Victor bomber; the de Havilland Trident waited in the wings. Meanwhile, Vickers at Weybridge had forged ahead of the field with its proposal as the V1000 and its VC7 airliner derivative, only to be set back by forces beyond its control.

V1000: Defeat from Vickers Victory

Kicking off in 1951 and running through to just beyond 1954, Vickers, under chief designer George Edwards and his men, began studies for a post-war military and civil long-range jet type. They were requested to frame the V1000 project by the Ministry of Supply (MoS) under Specification C.123D in 1952 as a new RAF type to replace the piston-powered, post-war types such as the Handley Page Hastings.

The resulting Vickers V1000 was designed to be far more than a Comet could ever be. V1000 was in effect a second-generation jet airliner before that era arrived. This aircraft represented a new, international outlook and design thinking, and came from the genius and vision of the men of Vickers led by George Edwards and the company's Advanced Projects Office under Ernest Marshall's leadership – the men who had created the Viscount and its 400+ global sales. Yet soon, the V1000 with the first airframe 85 percent complete was to be killed off by an insane decision taken by misguided politicians aided by BOAC's own machinations.

V1000 and its planned commercial, airline-specific derivative, the VC7, had it all – advanced design in structural and aerodynamic terms, a cranked swept wing,

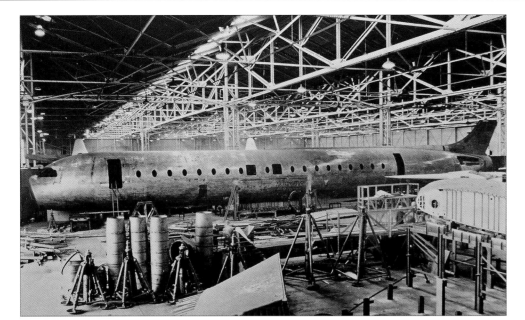

Close-ups of the in-the-metal V1000 prototype that was terminated at near 85 percent build. The cockpit window design motif was latterly seen in developed form on VC10.

four of the new jet turbofan power plants, long range, decent payload-range capacity and a runway performance that made it usable not just on long, straight runways near sea level, but on shorter and more difficult tropical fields on global airways which were specifically British in their end-of-empire conditions.

Only in its buried wing root engine installation was the V1000, in any sense, structurally different from the similarly shaped airframes that would soon come from Boeing, Douglas (and ultimately, Airbus). Burying the engines in the wing root was a highly aerodynamically efficient and fashionable design choice in the early jet age (as was the cranked wing): doing so offered significant aerodynamic benefits in comparison to having the engines hanging off the wing as pyloned pods where they

tended to cause unwanted turbulence and loss of lift by affecting the aerofoil's span-lift distribution efficiency, not to mention the leading-edge performance interrupting the slats or droops and doing the same to trailing edge flaps. These factors created design issues for the pylon-wing behaviours. Low hanging, wing-pylon engines also sucked up foreign objects from dirty runways and created a roll-angle limitation due to the risk of the ground striking the pods if a wing was too low in a cross-wind landing.

Yet engines buried in the wings (as also with the Comet) were a fire risk – being inside the wing structure and close to the fuselage and cabin. Buried engines were harder to work on too. VC10 would later answer the problem by podding its engines – but *not* from the vulnerable wing.

Right: The Tay Viscount was a Rolls-Royce Tay-engine powered jet Viscount of late 1948 and one of the earliest British civil jet airframes to be flown.

Below: Vickers Advanced Projects Office in 1957 with leader Ernie Marshall (centre) flanked by John Davis (left), Jack Swanson, Sammy Walsh and Maurice Wilmer.

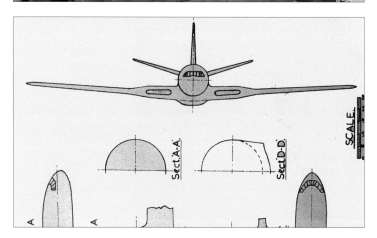

V1000 in plan drawings. Note the thin wing root (engines buried in situ) and wing box designs. Note typical Vickers tail dihedral not unlike that of the Viscount propliner.

The RAF's V1000 could have been in service by 1958, a VC7 perhaps by late 1959. The then Minister of Supply, Reginald Maudling, was originally keen on both and on Vickers as a company – after all V1000 was not (contrary to some latterly published claims) Vickers's first big jet – it had already learned much with the Valiant bomber.

The reason why V1000/VC7 was so needed was also obvious – the old British Empire and Commonwealth airfields were often hot in terms of local temperatures (>35°C) and high in terms of altitude (>5,000 feet), sometimes both. Headwinds and oceans also needed conquering. Long hauls and short hops were in the mix too.

Add in an aircraft's weight and you had the WAT formula of weight, altitude and temperature as one that determined if an airliner could get off the ground in the conditions and runway length available. Such tropical routes had runways of 5,000 to 6,000 feet in length, rarely perhaps 8,000 feet and often with dangerous local terrain. In contrast, New York and Los Angeles would soon offer 11,000- to 14,000-feet runway lengths at near-sea level. London Heathrow offered 10,500 feet. Even a flying boat could get airborne off such runway lengths, but a DC-8 60 series might struggle at full load.

Any new airliner to service the shorter tropical runway airfields and routes needed to be quick off the mark and able to climb properly – with decent payloads and some range. The same factors applied to the RAF's own transport uplift airframe requirements.

These tropical-type conditions applied across BOAC's route network except upon the North Atlantic routes, which were not then the principal focus of its earnings.

So, a machine for serving the military on Empire and Commonwealth routes could obviously serve the civilian airlines on the same medium-range routes. Here was a large sales opportunity for an aircraft

With a huge British military network to serve the world in the British Empire and Commonwealth route context, a fast, new RAF transport was needed; in fact, it was an urgent essential. That RAF transport type could also be built as an airliner in its own right. BOAC was invited to contribute to the V1000 airline transport variant specifications as an airline derivative was obvious – the VC7. But VC7 would give way to VC10. VC standing for Vickers Commercial, followed by a project number.

maker. Work on the project V1000 started in October 1952 with planed basic weight of around 100,000 lb. The RAF ordered six V1000s as a starting-off point. V1000, and therefore the airliner derivative VC7, was big, safe, had a swept wing with a low wing-loading. It was in every respect, notably structurally, far ahead of the Comet and technically in advance of the yet-to-be-delivered Boeing 707 in its original series.

With six-abreast seating as a design specification in 1953, the V1000 was also years ahead of the Boeing 707, that machine having to be expensively widened at late design and tooling stage to provide such seating configuration and airline economics.

But the 100–130-seat V1000 and VC7 were to be killed off by political decisions, national (state) funding decisions, confused directors and MPs and a curious mixture of agenda and circumstance. Claims were made by critics that it was overweight (it was not), that its Rolls-Royce Conway engines would not be able to be developed, yet exactly the same engine (the developed Conway) would power the rival Boeing 707 that BOAC quickly ordered once the home-grown Vickers big jet had been killed off.

The V1000 story was terminated by government decree on 24 October 1955 and the men of Vickers left to walk away, the toolings soon to be junked and the chapter closed. Vickers was left holding the remains of a still-born giant, what would have been the greatest airliner of its era.

Politicians tried to save the V1000/VC7, but it was not to be. Vickers' Sir George Edwards opined that the British had just handed the entire future world market for a new big jet airliner to the Americans.

This was loss of historic national significance, just as it would also be for the TSR2 airframe.

Britain's government had used (in great part, BOAC-framed) concerns over the V1000's engine power ratings and payload-range contentions to end the programme for an RAF-based original V1000 contract and thus the VC7 offshoot which Vickers had privately funded.

Vickers was less than 12 months behind schedule with V1000 – which was nothing compared to the delays of other airliner airframes, then and now. Yet delays were cited by enemies. But the RAF still needed a jet transport to keep up with its jet bombers and fighters – the problem was not going to go away. As for BOAC, soon after V1000 had been terminated, BOAC reputedly stated that as no British big jet was available, it would have to order the American one. Incredibly, faced with procurement delays, the government then asked Vickers if it could resurrect the V1000/VC7 project.

The answer was no.

This episode in British industrial and political history was a crash in procurement and policy of epic proportions.

The first V1000 /VC7 model defined its advanced, swept-wing scale.

Vanjet to VC10

Faced with the death of the V1000/VC7, chief designer Edwards continued a research and development programme in the field of the smaller, twin-engined or three-engined medium-range or intra-European 100-seat jetliner. Initially based on Vickers Viscount jet derivatives and then upon a Vanguard jet iteration also using some Valiant components (already paid for and tooled up), a Vanjet series of design proposals were framed across the mid-1950s. Vickers had tried a jet-powered version of their Viscount as early as 1949 when it mounted a Rolls-Royce Tay turbojet in a pod under each wing of a Viscount airframe.

The developments gave us the Vanjet, a machine designed to take on and beat the Sud Aviation Caravelle, the new French twin-jet regional airliner that was a soon-to-be a major sales success. Caravelle was good, but Vickers reckoned they could improve on its rather basic wing design by adding high-lift devices and better take-off performance.

Vickers decided to pursue the rear-mounted engine pylon–stub wing configuration seen on the Caravelle and created a series of two-, three- and four-engined Vanjet design proposals. Re-using Valiant or Vanguard parts to save time

Saunders Roe tested the V1000 model in its water tank for ditching characteristics. This resulted in the need to fit a nose-gear planning device to reduce diving effect on ditching.

An immediate jet-Viscount derivation was this swept-winged, swept-tail affair that utilized certain Viscount fuselage toolings to save money and time.

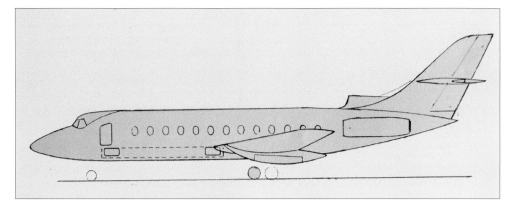

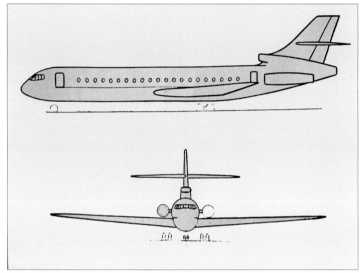

This far more conventional Vanjet idea is taken from Vanguard toolings with rear-mounted engines added.

and money was, in the main, soon to be abandoned as an idea.

Curiously, BOAC were now demanding propeller airliners, or prop-turbines like the long-range Britannia 312 with which to meet the future growth of passenger demand against the jet 707. Within months BOAC would order American jets – the 707 – over and above such prior choices, in the full knowledge that this aircraft (and not even its latter variants) would be unable to fully service BOAC's vital cashflow-earning tropical routes, due to its weak runway performance.

British companies such as Hunting, de Havilland, Bristol and Handley Page were all creating proposals for the regional jet – the small, 50–70-seat jet airliner with the potential to be stretched to a medium-range 100-seater. Naturally Vickers, having supplied BEA's Viscounts and hundreds of them to the world's airlines, wanted the business. Vanjet was detailed and tied down.

Yet the two- or three-engined Vanjet from Vickers was effectively killed off by political decisions taken around the British aircraft manufacturing industry (e.g. the Sandys Report) and the support given to the de Havilland Trident – a regional route tri-jet. Yet the British government decreed that with BOAC having just ordered the American 707, using vital foreign currency, the next new, big British airliners would have to be British-built. As such BOAC's

hands were now tied, but not, it should be noted, to Vickers, but to *any* viable British proposal – a vital point often missed by today's defenders of BOAC's actions. V1000 and VC7 were dead, so Vickers' only answer was to develop Vanjet into something bigger.

Vickers had little choice but to reinvent the Vanjet as a four-engined airliner as a sort of cousin of V1000 amalgamated into the Vanjet studies. So emerged the convoluted concept and design of what became the VC10 itself as son of V1000/VC7 and offspring of Vanjet.

There were over 80 paper studies for the Vanjets, all consuming not just time and resources, but Vickers's own money – *not* government funding. As for engines, Rolls-Royce Avon-29 engines would give way to early Conway 10s, soon to be developed.

Vanjet Specification B8613

In the later Vanjet idea of Specification B8613, the defining four-engined, 245,000-lb airframe with a payload of 34,000 lb and 3,500-mile range was suggested. Here was the first four-engined idea of the previously suggested three-engined Vanjet VC10. A cruising speed of 580 mph was cited. A cabin pressure differential of 8 psi would allow a 38,000-feet cruise. Wing sweep was 30 degrees but soon increased to 35 degrees.

The chosen T-tail design (with input from former Supermarine aerodynamicist and Vickers consultant Beverley Shenstone) was beneficially high and well swept; the horizontal tail and elevators were large, powered and effective, therefore reducing the risks of the deep stall phenomena.

The main wing leading-edge devices were also large and the wing (without engines hanging off it) was clean in aerodynamic terms. Use of Vanguard cockpit window tooling was latterly discarded except for the two main panels, resulting in the definitive VC10 windscreen and cockpit side-window design motifs. The engine nacelle/stub wing design was also highly advanced – to near-VC10 production status. The use and the expense of a new circular-section, keel-built, heavily reinforced fuselage was soon approved.

This was the four-engined officially labelled Vanjet VC10 in its first obvious

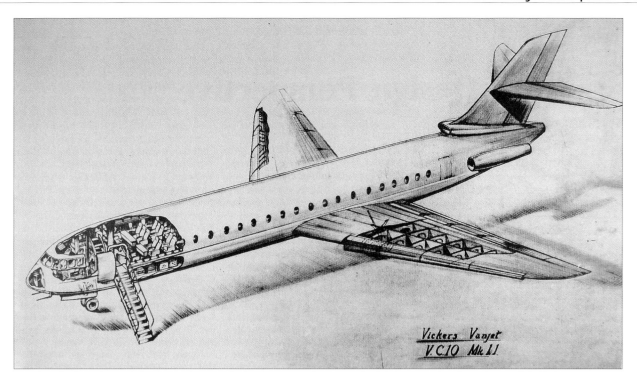

*Vickers Vanjet
V.C.10 Mk.11*

The very rare view of the defining, first-ever Vanjet VC10 type as labelled. A post-Sud Aviation Caravelle type, yet a more swept-winged, rear-engined tri-jet that was drawn up long before the DH Trident or Boeing 727. Note the large leading-edge devices even at this design stage.

iteration: it would become a swept-winged four-engined design with a 130-seat cabin. This was the defining moment of the VC10's genesis. The clean 35-degree sweep wing had a large leading-edge slat of long span with a greater degree of leading-edge angle than ever seen on any airframe at that time or until Boeing's 727 of a decade later.

First framed as Vanjet VC10 Mk.11 Drawing Series Number 79926, here was the penultimate step to the mighty V1100 specification VC10 – one step from a production design.

Of note, curiously, in 1959, a VC11, as a downscaled post-VC10, would be a strange, reverse-engineered suggestion for the BEA regional jet. It was abandoned as Vickers went for the BOAC long-haul jet order and amalgamation of the industry saw other projects (the Trident, and latterly the BAC1-11) given preference in the wheeling and dealing that created the British Aircraft Corporation after 1960.

So was born the VC10, but more recent claims that it was the only aircraft available to BOAC – thus ensuring its construction, and that its choice by BOAC was forced or not of BOAC's making – are in error, as both Bristol and Handley Page had viable jet airline transport design plans on the table and on show to BOAC. Even de Havilland offered a proposed Conway-engined Comet 4C+ which was not viable to re-engineer. A larger, new DH 118 four-jet proposal was also offered. Also on offer at this time was the Douglas DC-8 as the Douglas Company's version of the 707 concept.

The DC-8, like the earlier, original 707s had no wing leading-edge lift augmentation devices, so was very limited indeed in its

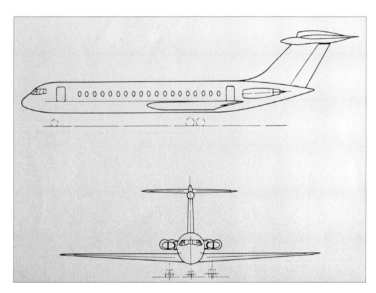

A four-engined development of the three-jet Vanjet VC10. Note the change to the tailfin and use of the T-tail. Vanguard fuselage and cockpit window frames still being suggested.

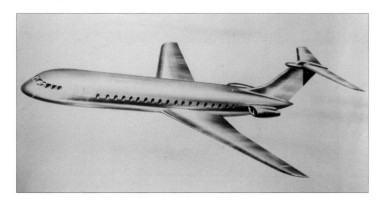

The VC10 begins to appear. A very rare Barry Jones original drawing for Vickers in 1956. Note the fin-top design and engine pods. Wingtips are of curved Kucheman type.

tropical route take-off performance. Boeing would soon spend many millions adding rather crude leading-edge lift mechanisms to its 707, then ultimately at vast cost, redesign the wing and leading-edge devices for higher lift in order to capture demanding airfield and tropical zone performance for airline appeal and sales.

Douglas would face lengthy and expensive delays to its DC-8's wing design even after launch and initial deliveries, and then have to redesign the engine pylons and the wing itself – yet never added extendable leading-edge devices.

Both these Boeing and Douglas airframes were available for order when BOAC ordered the VC10 (to its own tropical route specifications). Other companies, notably British ones, also had jetliner development projects to offer BOAC. But BOAC chose the VC10 of its own volition and used the Conway engine to keep the politicians happy. Actually Conway happened to be the biggest and most powerful, first true-bypass fan-type engine. So, its use was ensured by design not political power play.

With the Boeing 707 prototype flying and the DC-8 due, it seemed bizarre that British politicians should then argue that the new British four-engined airliner should be a direct copy of such machines, but argue this point they did. VC10 was too clever they suggested. But what on earth was the point of Britain building a 707 copy and why would foreign airlines order the British version over the original? Also, how would matching the 707 meet BOAC's very tough tropical route performance requirements as issued? And 707 could not meet such BOAC demands. It seems that a paradox of logic and internally inconsistent rationale infected the politics surrounding VC10.

There seemed to be a strange BOAC and government attitude in evidence. It appeared that Vickers would have to 'prove' that it could design and deliver the VC10 to very strict BOAC demands *before* the airline might offer real and total commitment

to the machine as orders. The ability to carry a 35,000-lb payload over a minimum 2,500-mile range at Mach 82–Mach 88 and to have full, high-temperature operating ability from unlengthened tropical-zone runways were the key BOAC demands.

Arguments of how many VC10 orders Vickers needed to make it viable, and who insisted on the numbers remain a debate today. Were, as BOAC claimed, 35 VC10s ordered in January 1958 (with an option for 20 more) with Vickers reputedly insisting on such numbers? It seems not. Vickers boss Edwards had stated that there was not a positive stand to demand an order for 35 VC10s and that this was a discussion number that reflected (and indeed was indicative of) BOAC's own claims that even with its 707 and VC10s as ordered, BOAC had stated that it would not have enough aircraft for the 1960s.

Vickers would need to build 75 VC10s to make a profit. It stated that there was no ultimatum to BOAC to order 35 VC10s and that increases in 1960s passenger and freight numbers, as predicted in BOAC's own official traffic analysis plan (after a dip in 1959 across BOAC and BEA), led to BOAC's suggestion, not just of needing 27 more airframes, but also of finding a way of meeting increasing freight demands. Hence the non-passenger VC10 pure-freighter variant that Vickers designed, and the cargo-door equipped VC10 passenger/freight combi as latterly delivered to EAA and BUA. By 1961, having claimed it had been forced into ordering the VC10, BOAC suddenly upped its VC10 order book and hinted at a larger version.

BOAC chose the VC10 and was as free to do so as it was to order Boeing 707s but with the political edicts that they should opt for the Rolls-Royce Conway that had suddenly become acceptable. Pan Am ordered 707s and a fleet of DC-8s. BOAC ordered Britannias, Comet 4s and then ordered nearly £50 millions worth of 707s despite its known weakness in take-off and range-payload abilities on the tropical routes that were vital revenue streams for BOAC.

Initially, in late 1957, BOAC (under the leadership of aviation leader Sir Gerard d'Erlanger) had enthused about the VC10 and dreams of an all-VC10 BOAC fleet were not so far-fetched as we might now think. By 1958, a £77-million contract for 35 VC10s plus 20 options was mooted. But BOAC was soon under new management and an all-707 fleet seemed far more likely. BOAC then manoeuvred and it was against this backdrop, and of BOAC's ever-changing orders for the VC10 and Super VC10, that changes took place. VC10 grew in size, then the much larger Super VC10 proposal was cut down in scale by BOAC to a half-way house specification. But BOAC did sign up to the VC10 project in 1958.

Ultimately, under yet another new BOAC chairman, Sir Giles Guthrie, BOAC may

Finally, the four-jet VC10 but note the shorter wings – to be much extended in span for the actual VC10 Type 1100 design.

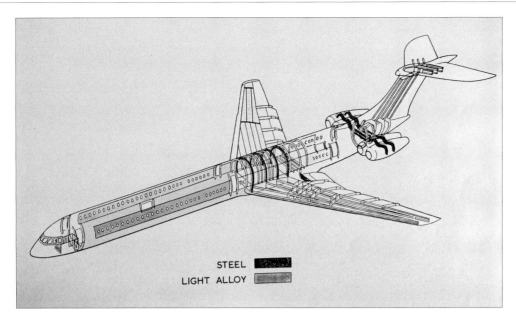

STEEL
LIGHT ALLOY

Left: VC10 monocoque with reinforcing beams, cradles and milled-from-solid window belt line – a unique design achievement for VC10. Note the overwing hoops and the tailfin supports.

Below: 14 January 1958. Sir George Edwards of Vickers (left) and BOAC's Sir Basil Smallpiece sign up for the VC10. Sir Basil is holding what might be the first VC10 model – a carved wooden scale version of VC10.

have got close to stopping Super VC10 in its tracks. What had been an order for 35 VC10s had drastically shrunk, with more Super VC10s ordered, but not enough to compensate for the lost Standard model VC10 orders. That order too was curtailed. What had started off as 45 VC10 orders had ended up as 15 VC10s and 30 Super VC10s, only then to be cut down to 10 VC10s and 30 Super VC10s. Then came Guthrie and cancellation of half that Super VC10 order, then all of it.

The on-off nature of BOAC's VC10 and Super VC10 orders endured through into Guthrie's final chop to the Super VC10 orders – only 17 to be built, alongside the 12 Standard VC10s.

The government then issued an aviation report as a White Paper, notably to discuss BOAC's costs and losses. The minister of the day (Amery) told the House of Commons that:

'The reason why there is no detailed reference to the VC10 in the White Paper is that no part of the deficit has resulted from the VC10 because it has not yet been introduced into service. It would be quite wrong to accept easily the idea that the VC10 was something pushed down the throat of the Corporation. It was not. I think that experience will show that this remarkable aircraft, the quietest aircraft in which I have ever flown, will prove a very great commercial success in a short time from now.'

The minister was very clear, contrary to BOAC's complaints and recent regurgitations, that VC10 had not been forced upon BOAC and, that prior to BOAC's complaints about the cost of operating the VC10s for which it had asked for and influenced so heavily, BOAC was losing a massive amount of money from its operations – which included having the Boeing 707 and the de Havilland Comet 4 in its fleet.

VC10 was, by 1963/64, plastered all over the national aviation media and the debate. The BOAC VC10 prototype G-ARTA

and the early BOAC machines were real. Super VC10s were being laid down. Surely the VC10 project could not be subjected to a V1000-style, last-minute termination as yet another project cancelled?

By 1964, Guthrie publicly criticized the VC10 and, in doing so, the VC10 and Super VC10 were damned in the eyes of the airline world and export market. The damage was probably incalculable. But Guthrie had been tasked with turning BOAC around and making it leaner and profitable.

No technical deficiency in the design or airframe was ever cited or evidenced. The nuances were more multi-layered. The key VC10 and Super VC10 benefits of passenger appeal, fuller load factor, slower safer take-offs and landings (also cheaper on tyres and brakes) and, of real note, lower maintenance and repair costs, were all lost in the haze of spin.

Into such circumstances was born the blameless VC10 – the aircraft BOAC asked for and specified in its operational requirements.

Amid the politics of the Super VC10 was a proposal for a double-decker Super VC10 with what would have ben the first jet airliner two-deck cabin. This is the Vickers/BAC artwork produced to promote the idea. State and private funding and orders were not forthcoming, but it would have been a true jumbo jet.

Applying Hindsight

We should in this new overview, note that the passage of time has further confused the VC10 story and that differing opinions and camps now exist. Yes, VC10 was overengineered and overweight, but only as a result of meeting its very demanding customer-led specification. The brilliant tri-jet airliner, the Boeing 727, was also overwinged and overengined in order to meet its performance targets of tough operating conditions in the USA and beyond. Yet when did you ever hear any criticism of it for such design and performance abilities? So why was the VC10 attacked for doing the same thing and at the very requirements of the airline that ordered it? As for BEA and its own curtailment of the high-lift, wing-equipped, 100-150-seat early D.H. Trident proposal with potential Rolls-Royce Medway engines, well, the 727 picked up where the shortened and derated Trident (at BEA's behest) cut its own sales and operational throat. The initial VC10 prototype Type 1100 emerged from Vickers' construction hall at Brooklands on 15 April 1962. After ground tests up to V1 speed, the first flight was on 29 June 1962, with chief test pilot Jock Bryce at the controls assisted by test pilots, Brian Trubshaw and Bill Cairns. The first production machine as the BOAC Type 1101 for BOAC took off from Brooklands short runway on 8 November 1962 flown by Trubshaw.

Before and after that event, the VC10 meanwhile was, and remains, subject to years of claim and counter claim about its procurement and its abilities. Recent historians have cited the records found in the National Archives (of Britain) to support a view that was kinder to BOAC and its decisions over VC10. Regretfully, even academic-level VC10 researchers and commentators have fallen for the evidence found in the National Archives.

Such evidence suggests that BOAC were forced into buying the VC10 by the British Government, and that no other potential British aircraft designs for the specified task were planned or available, which is inaccurate on both counts. At face value BOAC's records in these archives present a plausible position, but it seems that such records are allegedly contaminated and constructed with political and corporate spin in order to present a narrative on behalf of some in the anti-VC10 camp of the time. Reputations needed protecting it seems.

No less a figure than the famous airline transport luminary, aerodynamics expert and electronics systems pioneer, Peter Hearne (also once a leader of the Royal Aeronautical Society as President RAeS 1980–1981), gave voice to such an opinion of spin being found in the BOAC records. He categorically framed errors in the records and the BOAC bias within them, and stated that the V1000 (and VC10 story) as framed by such documents, were the subject of spin – not of an aerodynamic kind, but of a corporate-speak kind.

In 2008 Hearne wrote in *The Aeroplane*, that he had worked in the early 1950s inside the BOAC jet airliner development unit – commenting that BOAC had spent time and money on jet airliner studies, prior to suddenly then deciding to support prop-turbine-powered airliners (the Bristol Britannia and its faction) for the late 1950s and into the 1960s as its next procurement needs. Hearne left BOAC amid such confusion and as V1000 was about to be sabotaged by many parties and agendas, not least BOAC.

According to Hearne (whom the author subsequently interviewed) as a luminary who was there at the original time, the records appeared contaminated, yet today, others are prepared to cite them as referenced fact that are definitive of how it was. Yet surely such facts were reframed versions serving a specific position as seen from a BOAC and a politically framed reputational standpoint.

BOAC was, said Hearne, principally responsible for the confused and contradictory airframe and power plant decisions over V1000 and subsequent jet procurement.

BOAC also stated at the time that the VC10 required further development for use on non-tropical routes, and why should BOAC be party to yet more risky, post-Comet airliner development? But hang on, BOAC had asked for VC10 to be designed for tropical routes, not non-tropical (mostly Atlantic) routes. This was the bizarre and contradictory argument of the twisting and turning that took place at the time.

Why blame the development costs of turning an airliner into something you did not ask to be designed in the first place. Further, if it was all well and good for BOAC to support the Comet 1 and Comet 4 design, development and service use as part of supporting Great Britain's national interest, why is the argument now made that it was wrong to suggest or ask that BOAC support the same aims by ordering the VC10 – not least for tropical routes that neither 707 or DC-8 could adequately service?

Anti-VC10 commentators often forget to mention that BOAC converted £50 million of vital British currency into US dollars to order its 707s, and that Britain had few cash reserves left in age of post-war near bankruptcy and restricted foreign currency spending. So the next British airliner procurement had to be spent in British currency inside the national economy – whomever that airliner might be ordered from. Once again the VC10 is absolved from BOAC's so-called forced hand over the VC10 that the aircraft's critics' cite.

Let's not forget that the £50 million spend on 707 orders, was for an airliner that could not properly perform or deliver on BOAC's key tropical routes. But you hear less about that from the today's VC10 commentators who prefer to rely on the contents of the National Archives.

Historians still ask us to absolve BOAC of blame. Yes, BOAC was encouraged to support VC10 by the hand of government but BOAC was the body that looked at several proposals from Handley Page, Bristol, de Havilland, and Vickers, only to choose the Vickers proposal that BOAC had stated was 'viable' for tropical routes.

Vickers finally received some state funding (under £10 million) towards VC10 development and into Super VC10, but only after it had spent millions of its own money on V1000/VC7, Vanjet and the VC10 precursor studies.

But did BOAC curtail or compromise its own wishes? Many say no. Others point out that BOAC had a less-than-visible pro-Boeing agenda.

BOAC's critics have always referred to the BOAC 'Boeing Boardroom' but this is too simplistic to cite without wider evidence. However, few of today's observers are aware that one of BOAC's top 1950s directors (serving BOAC from 1947 to 1957 even as managing director and executive vice-chairman) was Air Commodore Whitney Straight MC.

Straight, ostensibly English, and resident in England, was in fact an American born of high society, power and influence and a cousin of C. V. Whitney a former chairman of Pan American Airways. No wonder some theorists suspected a pro-American, pro-Boeing agenda at BOAC during the crucial years when V1000 was killed off and VC10 was reluctantly ordered, then criticised.

BOAC's 1950s long haul airliner design and development department, once it abandoned the idea of a jet type in the early 1950s (amid the Comet 1 debacle), aligned itself to the Bristol Aircraft Company, Sir Peter Masefield, and its prop-propelled Britannia.

It later decided to abandon them too, and go for Boeing and a jet one at that. These were BOAC-created internal inconsistencies that had nothing whatsoever to do with the VC10.

Vickers do appear to have under estimated the design and development costs of the VC10, which cannot be ignored. However, this is a tangent to the actual landscape of the airliner's customer-defined operating requirements and performance, and BOAC's inconsistencies amid its own demands. Given just how many chiefs and senior managers and directors BOAC had, it would surely be wrong to blame Vickers for BOAC's very concerning financial position – which existed before the VC10 ever flew in BOAC colours. Government Air Minister Amery pointed this out during public debate about BOAC's financial position that took place prior to VC10's introduction.

BOAC's Comet 4 operations were costing them a lot of money on a seat-per-mile

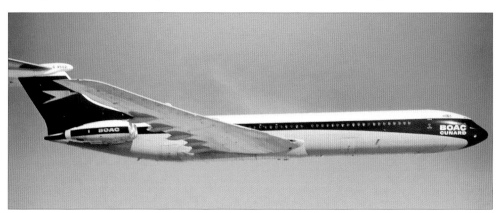

BOAC briefly teamed up with the Cunard Company to promote a blue-riband transatlantic service to meet rising fly-and-cruise demand. Hence the BOAC CUNARD titles applied in gold to the Super VC10 as seen here in a classic BOAC publicity shot of the era.

and payload-to-range accounting basis. Remember, Comet 4 carried less than 80 passengers in BOAC configuration but used four thirsty engines and flew on multi-stop long-range services with massive operating costs.

Surely the government did not twist BOAC's arm into the VC10? Some say it did, but the evidence is not conclusive by any means. Other airliner projects existed too. If the T-tail had not fallen off the Handley Page Victor, perhaps its seriously proposed and drawn up airliner derivative might have been chosen over VC10. And what of a re-engined Comet 5? It was proposed and BOAC knew about it.

BAC and the politics of the time

The VC10 researcher cannot ignore that in 1960 Vickers was about to be absorbed into the new amalgam that was the British Aerospace Corporation (BAC). Cancelling VC10 and Super VC10 as that event occurred would have both commercial and political implications beyond BAC.

As men like BOAC's leaders – d'Erlanger, then Smallpiece, then Slattery, (then Guthrie with his 1964 Guthrie Plan to terminate the entire VC10/Super VC10 run) and their co-leaders, and a host of civil servants and politicians (notably Sandys, and then Amery) would discover, VC10, Super VC10, BOAC, and the arrival of the politically driven outcome of merger in the British aircraft industry as BAC, was a rolling snowball of demands and potential disaster.

Some authors claimed (as if to absolve BOAC) that there were problems with the VC10s performance. This is another act of alleged spin. Like all advanced new aircraft, VC10 had some issues at prototype stage that needed to be resolved and solutions found, such as the higher-than-expected drag and the need for some minor wing design revisions. Such revisions were little compared to the major aerodynamics, wing design and tooling changes made to the 707 and in even greater extent to the DC-8 before and during early production series. Yet now we see the VC10 development issues (all solved) being cited as problems with performance, which however did not exist into airline or RAF service.

Through such claims there is further evidence of an anti-VC10 agenda that seems to confabulate things to the advantage of another agenda.

VC10 met all its performance claims and exceeded several of them.

Such are the many streams and strings of the VC10 story over which so many have argued for so long.

Here in this VC10 narrative, the differing claims and contexts are cited. The reader can reach his or her own conclusion.

The author has spoken to several of the main players (including Edwards, Trubshaw, Hearne and BOAC sources) and has reached the view that as Brian Trubshaw stated, BOAC got what it asked for.

Even before its first flight, VC10 therefore flew into a headwind of pre-judgement and prejudice. Yes, BOAC had to juggle the consequences of its own actions and claims, against the fact that it was bringing a major new British aircraft into service and expecting its flight crews and cabin crews to embrace the new airliner with enthusiasm and commitment as employees. But BOAC's constant late 1950s/early 1960s manoeuvrings and claims and internal inconsistencies of argument do – when examined and seen as a whole, not a cherry-picked argument – reveal that the VC10 was not at fault.

BOAC had a pro-jet, then a pro-prop-turbine strategy, then an anti-V1000/VC7 airframe position, then an anti-Rolls-Royce Conway engine position, only then to order the Boeing 707 with such Conway engines and in the full knowledge that the 707 could not meet BOAC's tropical route demands. BOAC went on to choose a potential Vickers VC10 specification, call it economically viable, ask Vickers to develop it, and then try to run away from it as fast as it could.

Yet we are told BOAC was apparently almost blameless and caught in the whims of government and that no other British projected airliner designs existed – which is patently untrue.

Brian Trubshaw and Peter Hearne were both correct. BOAC chose and framed VC10 for its tropical routes and then changed its mind – amid a record of mind-changing, that included internal BOAC preferences and choices, taking little cognizance of the State, government, public and political pressure as the new British Aircraft Corporation itself was formed within the revolving doors of British politics and men of power.

Years after the early 1960s bashing that BOAC administered to the VC10, when the truth came out, the facts were rather interesting.

Contrary to BOAC's pro-Boeing bleatings, the VC10 fleet, notably the Super VC10 fleet (Super VC10 being directly comparable to the BOAC Boeing 707-336 type), offered similar costs to run, much higher utilisation through higher daily flying hours, more seats filled per flight and lower maintenance and repair costs. BOAC's Standards and Supers flew higher revenue earning hours than any other airliner in the BOAC fleet. Published IATA figures categorically showed a long-term increased VC10 and Super VC10 load factor of passenger preference to the types, long after the introduction of the service.

BOAC became British Airways in 1974 and operated its last VC10 service on 29 March 1981, having carried 13 million passengers without accident.

Conversely, BOAC had lost two Boeing 707s in service.

Engineering Excellence

Left: The massive cockpit or flight deck was much bigger than the rival Boeing 707's and more spacious for the crew. Note the deep windows for better visibility.

Below: Detail of the centre console, thrust levers and main instruments.

Expertly designed, artisan built and created to perform like no other, VC10 was proof of British engineering integrity. Brand-new VC10 airframes lifted off from Brooklands' very short runway at first flight in well under 2,500 feet, to fly on to Vickers Wisley airfield base for testing and fitting-out.

Vickers' Sir George Edwards operated a truly integrated team of experts. The resultant quality of their designs and products were world class and world beating. It is not possible here to mention every employee of the advanced projects design office, the engineering projects teams and the vital shop floor workers, but we can, for the record, cite leading VC10 project contributors.

Ernest E. Marshall led the Vickers design function under Sir George Edwards's leadership, Basil Stevenson was Assistant Chief Designer, Hugh Hemsley was Assistant Chief Engineer and VC10 project engineering leader, Hugh Tyrer was Vickers' Chief Metallurgist. Jack Swanson and Ted Chivers were the senior draughtsmen. Frank Ward, Sammy Walsh, Maurice Wilmer and John Davis were lead contributors in the advanced projects team.

VC10 nose and flight deck structure seen uncovered: built like a battleship and very different from Boeing and Douglas nose and fuselage design and construction. The rival 707 had an internal structural reinforcing post beside each pilot's side-window.

The aerodynamics team – the VC10's aero men under Ken Lawson as Chief Aerodynamicist, saw John Hay as Assistant Chief Aerodynamicist, Mike Salisbury as Assistant Lead Aerodynamcist, Roger Back and Heinz Vogel as aerodynamicists. Dieter Kuchemann was a project contributor via his RAE role.

The engineering team saw David McElhinney as Chief Stress Engineer, David James as Chief Structures Engineer, John Davies as Chief Weights Engineer and Jim Richards Deputy Chief Stressman, while David Findlay was Leader Wing Stress. The fuselage Project Manager was Maurice Wilmer and Alec Paterson fuselage build leader.

The engineering systems team, covering the innovative flight controls, and electrical systems men, included Ted Petty as Chief Project Engineer and Harry Zeffert as Leader Electrical Engineering.

The flight-test teams for VC10 and Super VC10 were G. R. 'Jock' Bryce, Brian Trubshaw, Bill Cairns, John Cochrane, Eddie McNamara, Doug Howley, Roy Mole, Chris Mullen, Roy Holland, Ian Muir and Peter Diss. Later Super VC10 and RAF development airframe flight crews included R. Radford and P. Baker. Vickers training pilots to BOAC and VC10 customers were D. Hayley-Bell and L. Roberts, with D. Ackery in the flight test department.

Design Demands

Lift and lifting ability were the crucial factors for the VC10 and they would firstly come from wing design. Thus were set the VC10s key aerodynamic design parameters. Then came the new fail-safe split-systems control design philosophy, the electrical and service systems innovations and then the structural design ingredients.

All of these advanced airframe and systems developments combined to create a next step in large airliner design and many of the VC10's features and achievements can now be seen in recent Boeing and Airbus airframes

VC10 needed to be stronger and more fatigue-resistant than the Comet or an airliner designed for easier routes. Rough runways in Africa would demand a very tough structure that would resist fatigue. Over 55 percent of the VC10's structure (by weight) was machined from high-quality, solid lumps or slabs (billets) of metal. This delivered safe sections of very strong, large aircraft parts in the wings, fuselage and inner chassis structure of consistent metallurgical quality. A smoother exterior finish (aerodynamically beneficial) was also a benefit of the expensive machining process for the alloys used: VC10's skin smoothness criteria was the best in the world. And with a reduced panel and parts count, construction was easier and torsional rigidity higher – with less joints and rivets to flex or fail or corrode.

Often unreferenced in VC10 history was the VC10's very small pressure bulkhead and its angled mounting – both deliberate design features intended to reduce stress on the bulkhead which was a key pressurized airframe component and safety factor.

A VC10 wooden mock-up was initially built and then test-section airframe sections (non-flying) completed as CN 801A/801/B/801/2 as nose, forward fuselage (structural test) and tail, respectively. These were used to validate numerous design aspects and the cabin pressure differential upon the structure.

The main wing skins were machined from single bits of metal 35 feet long – much stronger than a multiple panel skin. VC10's main wing had only seven main panels – ensuring great consistency of strength. Upper wing surfaces were made of a zinc-rich alloy and the lower surfaces of an aluminium copper alloy. The three-part wing structure was therefore very strong indeed and so too was the central wing box that carried many loadings.

With no engines on the wing (unlike the 707) to offer weight and dynamic relief forces on the wing structures, the VC10's clean wing had to be stiffer, stronger and heavier. This is one of the reasons that the VC10 is more expensive to operate than a 707, because the VC10's wing structure is slightly heavier for the same number of passengers accommodated, with figures of 25.7 percent of maximum take-off weight (MTOW) as opposed to the 707-320's 24.6 percent.

However, it was soon obvious in flight testing that two drag issues were extant – that of confused airflow around the engine exhausts and that the wingtip vortex was stronger than was anticipated from the wind tunnel tests. The prototype aircraft seemed to produce more drag than predicted and in some cases buffet (localized flow separation) was encountered. Localized flow reversal under the engine nacelles was even suggested by observed tuft-testing in-flight. So, in original prototype configuration the VC10 had a small drag-related performance

With flaps and slats hanging and gear down, the elegance of RAF C.Mk.1 XV107 as delivered in December 1967, shows off the changes to the Standard Type 1100 VC10 configuration incorporated into the original RAF VC10s: Super VC10-type wings, longer engine stub support wings, more power and a tailcone with an APU. The extra freight door is not visible.

issue and quick changes to the design had to be made – at Vickers' expense. The revised wingtips and added beaver tail-type fairings were fitted to the back of the engines – fine tuning exhaust and local airflow patterns.

G-ARTA, the manufacturer's prototype, and in 1963 BOAC customer airframe G-ARVE were both used for testing and curing these problems, with G-ARVE then being refurbished, prior to delivery as new to BOAC on 1 October 1964.

The VC10 wing aerofoil had a new shape – with a flatter top and more cambered lower profile at the wing root – in direct contrast to the 707's old-style top-curved aerofoil. The VC10 had a new design of aerofoil which needed development.

Subsequent changes to the aerofoil, notably to Super VC10 design, indicate that this was less of an error by Vickers and more of a case of discovery during the design of a new theory upon which the VC10 was the first airliner for which this wing profile was specifically designed. For this, Vickers worked together with the National Physical Laboratory (NPL), the Royal Aircraft Establishment (RAE) and also the Aircraft Research Association (ARA) and they designed a wing with a peaky pressure distribution. This was so named as the aerofoil produced a low-pressure peak over the leading edge as opposed to the previous theory of a fairly constant low-pressure section over a significant portion of the wing's aerofoil chord.

The original VC10 wingtip design was of square type but revised to Kuchemann standard – adding to the total span. After flight testing, a new, tall, inboard wing fence would be added to control spanwise airflow near the stall speed and benefit engine intake flow – all at minor cost to

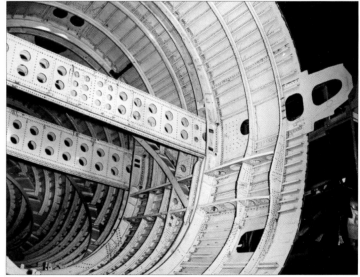

the lift coefficient from the small reduction in the wing's upper surface area. The tall inboard fence was insisted upon by the Vickers test pilots to improve handling margins. VC10 had to be proven deep-stall safe and risky testing took place – but the wing performance was benign and soon finalized.

The BOAC 'early wing' VC10 Type 1101 variants were slightly less economical than the latterly modified Type 1102/1103 airframes, but BOAC had declined to include the various improvements that were suggested – although incorporating the changes would have delayed delivery. The BOAC specification VC10 still managed to fulfil all the promises made with regard to the hot-and-high runway performance that were requested by BOAC – contrary to some erroneous later claims.

The Super VC10 saw the engines moved a further 11 inches (27 cm) outboard from

Rear fuselage reinforcements: massive engine bearer beams and hooped tail load carriers amid extra-thick frames and cleats.

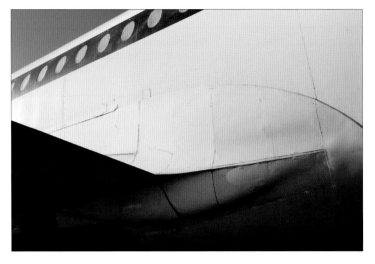

Above: Changes to the VC10/Super VC10 wing saw a revised leading edge and this fence added to reduce span-wise flow.

Right: Vickers put a lot of work into the wing-to-fuselage conjunction fillet to reduce drag. Anti-tear straps are visible on the fuselage structure.

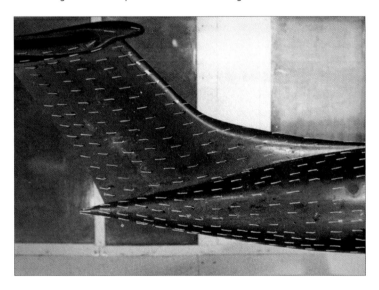

Above: The elegant streamlined tail in all its industrial design glory. The tailplanes are as big as a small fighter jet's main wing. Early BOAC livery is depicted on G-ARVC prior to engine fairings being added. Note the curved lower fin rudder section trailing-edge shape – changed to angular on the Super VC10.

Above right: Wind tunnel work with tuft-testing helped solve the T-tail aerodynamic issues and proved the need for a very tall, swept tail to reduce deep-stall risks.

the fuselage and tilted by 3 degrees, and a step in the stub-wing engine mount section in order to reduce local airflow interference and resultant drag eddies. Standard VC10 G-ARVE was used for the first flight trials of this modification but it was put back into normal VC10 specification prior to delivery to BOAC.

T-tail

The VC10's most obvious feature was its streamlined design and curved tailfin and tailplane design.

Of significance was the decision to employ a T-tail configuration, the advantages of which included better (increasing) control authority compared to a low-set tail at high-incidence angles, a beneficial end-plate effect upon fin drag, and helpful effects in critical Mach numbers with a better ability to balance increased main-wing chord. The high fin also removed the tailplanes from the issues of engine exhaust-flow plumes and engine-pod flow and compressibility and interference effects in rear-mounted engine configurations. Only the spectre

of the deep-stall or super-stall with its potential for loss of elevator authority and resulting locked-in irrecoverable total airframe stall, haunted the T-tail as a design philosophy. Most manufacturers relied on a control stick-pusher to avoid a too nose-high attitude. VC10 had one by legislative order, but its T-tail was unique in avoiding the worst aspects of the T-tail stall behaviours and characteristics due to its sweep and height, allied to massive elevators that were properly powered. There was never a VC10 deep-stall accident, unlike other T-tail airliner airframes.

The tailfin had vertical spars that grew from deep within the fuselage tail structure and vertical stingers and a very thick skin sheeting, all combining to resist twist and failure.

With the VC10's engines mounted from a stub wing from the fuselage – rather than wing pylon – the VC10 Conway application required a new way of mounting components

The classic VC10 tail in BOAC Speedbird colours. Much of the VC10 and Super VC10 aerodynamics research was carried out in the wind tunnel at the R.A.E. Bedford facility.

A very unusual view showing off the vital main wing torsion box side where the wing would join. VC10 really was built like a Vickers battleship or submarine – heavy metal.

The beaver tail exhaust fairings were added after prototype flight testing to solve the drag issue. There were in fact three differing exhaust/beaver tail designs tried out and applied across the various production versions.

The Super VC10 engine stub wing was 11 inches longer than the Standard-type VC10 and had a 3-degree angle revision.

Main gear was angled back by 10 degrees and fitted with anti-lock braking and an air compressor. Allied to wing-ground effect, this gave the VC10 a very smooth landing behaviour.

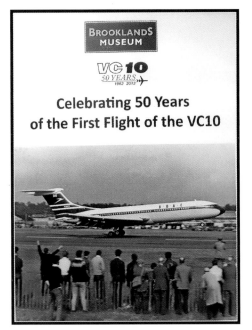

Prototype G-ARTA lifts off on its first flight from Brooklands in 1962. Commemorated in 2012 at Brooklands itself by the Brooklands Museum Trust.

to or from it using a central mounting 'carrier' beam. Each engine was contained in its own 'bay' with a firewall to stop or contain fire and escaping engine debris damage to the neighbouring engine – a vital safety factor. Further external strapping would latterly be added.

Conway CO12/540
Max thrust at take-off: 20,370 lb (9,240 kg) x 4
Max continuous thrust: 16,560 lb
Cruise thrust: 4,500 lb at 35,000 ft with specific fuel consumption of 0.823 lb per hour
Max pressure ratio: 15:1
Dry weight: 5,001 lb
Length: 54 in
Engine diameter: 51 in

Note: Super VC10 and RAF VC10 used Conway 550B (21,825 lb/988 kg) x 4. The 24,000-lb thrust version not optioned.

VC10 Specification Type 1101-1102-1103
Length: 158 ft 8 in/48.46 m
Span: 146 ft 2 in/44.56 m
Height: 39ft 5in/12.04 m
Wing area: 2,851 ft²/264.9 m²
MTOW: 312.000 lb/141,520 kg
Powerplant: Rolls-Royce Conway 42/540 x 4 at 21,000-lb static thrust each
Speed: 590 mph
Range: 5,500 mi/8,850 km
Capacity: 135–151 seats

Note* Types 1102-1103 with revised wing and tips.
Note** Cargo door offered to Types 1102/3, 1106, and Type 1154 Super VC10.

VC10/ Super VC10 Firsts

- Fail-safe design concept and structure.
- Use of solid metal billets and milled one-piece structural members.
- Reinforced fuselage keel and major cabin apertures.
- Smaller pressure bulkhead mounted at an angle.
- Copper-rich aluminium alloys and titanium alloys used in structure.
- Four-rear mounted engines on stub wings.
- Advanced high-lift clean main wing with big slat angle/area.
- Multiple redundancy operating and mechanical split-systems.
- Improved cabin airflow and comfort.
- New standards of corrosion protection.
- Developed CAT1-CAT2-CAT3 Autoland and Dunlop anti-skid braking.
- Developed carbon brakes (latterly used on Concorde).
- Super VC10 used new, advanced technology wing design.

Many VC10 metal panels were larger – so were stiffer and had fewer rivets and joints. The Vickers designers reduced the traditionally deployed numbers of lap joints, splices and seams along the window line – instead using a machined from solid panel along the entire length of the window belt line. The window line panels were 34 feet by 6 feet and ¾ inches thick. There were fewer crack-raising points and stiffening was integral – not add-on. Diagonally located load support beams, torque boxes and massive cleating, all created a really strong structure. The additional skin cleats at each frame station would restrict any failure to one frame bay. Channel frames were doubled up with overlapping edges and the fuselage panels were laid transversely over their frames and with circumferential straps over them.

The crucial wing box and centre section – leading back to the very heavily reinforced tail area – was where VC10's real heavy metal and strength was to be found.

VC10's first flight in 1962 meant that it had two years of development flying before entering BOAC service and prior to certification the VC10 flew 4,230 hours of test flying. Vickers and the BOAC VC10 development crew flew over 4,000 hours of testing with G-ARTA. BOAC's men, who spent a lot of time at Wisely, included captains Cane, Gray, Phillips, Rendall and Stoney, all either ex-Imperial or RAF and with Comet 1 and 4 experience. BOAC's top man, Captain Norman Bristow as flight commander, became the face of the BOAC VC10 and Super VC10 flight teams, alongside another Norman, Captain N. Todd. BOAC pilots overseeing earlier VC10 progress were captains H. J. Field, A. P. W. Cane and R. Knights. The

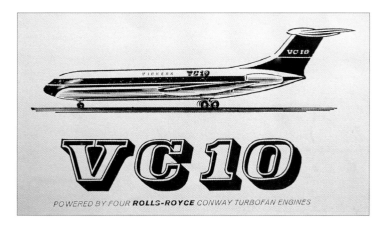

A lovely piece of early Vickers/BAC VC10 manufacturer's marketing material.

Inside Brooklands main VC10 build hall is this unusually liveried BOAC Super VC10, the first Super, but sporting the VC10 logo and the earlier BOAC lettering.

Going up! In the early blue and gold of BOAC with stepped cheatline, G-ARVM powers out of Brooklands from a sub-2,000-feet take-off run to VR point. The steep climb angle was a VC10 hallmark, unmatched by any big contemporary jet.

Canadian, Captain J. Futcher, was a well-known senior VC10 commander who was in charge of the hijacked BOAC Super VC10 at Dawson's Field and was officially recognized for his actions. Captain Peter Cane was BOAC's chief liaison with Vickers during the design and flight proving programme for the VC10. Captain Tom Stoney would travel the same VC10 journey as flight manager, and captains M. Majendie and J. Nicholls would be the VC10 chief training officers. Captain L. Heron would also be part of the BOAC VC10 development process.

After many months route proving and testing of flight capabilities in Africa, Spain and colder climes, BOAC and its crews mustered for the VC10's entry into service at its London Heathrow Airport base.

VC10 went, as ordered, onto BOAC's MRE or Medium Range Empire routes that defined the route BOAC structure; the BOAC Far East routings were titled as Dragon Routes.

BOAC's VC10 offered Economy Class accommodation from 135 to 151 seats dependent on how many seats were First Class and the overall seat pitch. Super VC10 seated 163 to 174 but BOAC offered 16 seats in First Class – soon reduced to 12 or less if the front cabin mail/freight cage was included.

This rare view of a BOAC Super VC10 in construction at the Vickers Brooklands Weybridge site shows off the thickness of the heavy gauge metal work around the cockpit window frames. The smooth fuselage skin finish is also evident.

Into the Air: BOAC

The first commercial BOAC VC10 flight was commanded by Captain A. M. Rendall on 29 April 1964. BOAC used stops at Frankfurt or Rome on the Nigeria service and from such beginnings VC10s began to replace Comet 4 and Britannia 312 equipment on BOAC's routes in Africa – notably down via Nairobi on the lucrative Johannesburg service.

From 1965 to 1969 BOAC used its Standard VC10s to build up a Middle East route network to service the growing economies of the region. Some VC10 routes from London went to Rome or Zurich, thence to Tel Aviv or Beirut, then onwards to the Gulf States and India.

Sometimes overlooked were the BOAC VC10/Super VC10 and BUA/BCAL VC10 forays into South America – Lima and Caracas being favourites.

The Super VC10 (manufactured 1965–1970) was the biggest airframe in Europe and the strongest, fastest and most powerful civil airliner built and flown anywhere at that time, a true second-generation airliner.

The BOAC-branded Super VC10 entered service on 1 April 1965 with Captain Norman Todd at the controls on the daily premier London Heathrow–New York JFK run. G-ASGD Golf Delta opened up the route and soon extended it down to the BOAC Caribbean destinations. Boston, Bermuda and Toronto were all Super VC10 destinations – with service to the US West Coast planned, but at that time still the preserve of the longer-ranged BOAC 707-436 machines. The 707s were replaced on the runs to Chicago as early as 1966 by Super VC10.

VC10 and Super VC10 had massive appeal. Figures from the International Airline Transport Association (IATA) for April 1965–May 1966 show that the BOAC Super VC10 services in comparison with a basket of 14 other airlines that operated Boeing 707 and Douglas DC-8 services, had a load factor advantage of 20–25 percent on a consistent basis and even a lowest advantage of 10 percent (November 1965). Such was the stuff of the appeal of the BOAC VC10 fleet. Even after BOAC introduced its first 747-100s on the transatlantic routes, passengers still preferred the 'gold standard' Super VC10 service – despite the lack of in-flight visual entertainment. VC10 and Super VC10 built an enduring passenger appeal that was worth millions to BOAC in seats sold, yet rarely cited in accountants' figures.

What the Pilots Thought

The VC10 pilots all agreed – saying things that reflected their genuine love of flying an airliner that handled, said some, like a jet fighter. Boeing 707 pilots who flew a VC10 were astounded at the differences in performance and handling – especially with an engine out.

VC10 pilots observed that their aircraft was:

"Incredible to fly."

"Huge performance and safety reserves."

"You knew it would not bite you, and that it could also get you out of a nasty situation."

"VC10. It was utterly viceless. Engine out was easy."

The classic colours on the classic airframe. BOAC style on the Super VC10.

BOAC Super VC10 going up. Hit VR and then attack the sky with the Conways at full power if you could spare the fuel.

G-ARVB in the VC10's early BOAC colours and seen during flight testing prior to the inboard wing fence being standardized.

"Much easier to fly than a 707, especially if you lost an engine, and even more so if that occurred shortly after take-off."

Such were the comments of VC10 pilots – even Comet 4 pilots coming over to the new BOAC machine were taken aback at the ability and ease of the VC10. One of BOAC's lead VC10/Super VC10 training commanders was the ex-wartime RAF bomber pilot Tom Stoney. He said of VC10: "It was really terribly easy to fly. Only that narrow undercart needed watching in crosswinds. VC10 was so safe, and almost flew itself down the ideal glide path to arrive at such a slow speed compared to the Boeing."

Captain Ronald Ballantine recalled that the VC10: "Flew like a dream, a fighter-type performance. Stable, safe and with far less deep-stall worries than other types. BOAC crews were rightly proud to fly it and, of course, we never lost one."

Captain James L. Heron was a member of the VC10 development crew and co-authored the BOAC VC10 flying manual yet his name is rarely cited in VC10 literature. An Australian, he had flown the Consolidated Liberator for the RAF, and Lockheed Constellations and Bristol Britannias for BOAC before transferring to the VC10 fleet. He was also on board the Super VC10 inaugural flight LHR–JFK on 1 April 1965 captained by Harry R. Nicholls. James Heron retired in 1971 with a BOAC seniority number of Three. Captain Heron's son once asked his father which aircraft, of all the numerous types he had flown in a career which spanned 44 years, was his favourite. James Heron answered without hesitation: "The VC10. It truly was superb."

The BOAC VC10 fleet captain was Norman Todd who loved the aircraft. He went on to fly Concorde and opined that the VC10 was not just utterly brilliant, but a good training ground for Concorde pilots.

Christopher Orlebar flew the VC10 and then Concorde and prior to his death worked with the reserved VC10s at Brooklands Museum. "Simply the best handling and best performing four-engined jet this side of Concorde. We felt so safe," said Orlebar.

VC10 and Concorde test pilot (Chief Test Pilot BAC) Brian Trubshaw was clear: "The feel of the VC10 flight controls was superb – artificially created but utterly realistic and accurate. Despite the weight and the carved from solid structure, she was light to handle. A firm pull on the stick got her off and up very quickly. Then it was that

amazing climb angle until you throttled back, the fuel gauges swung down to a better flow rate and once cleaned up, VC10 and Super VC10 just cleaved along. Losing an engine was no big deal."

Comfort Class

First Class was typical of its era with big seats that reclined into almost-beds and service was of course superb with champagne, caviar and cigars aplenty.

A VC10 hallmark was the superior quality and comfort of the Economy Class cabin – a new seat design built with single spar, with a one-piece moulded construction that could be wiped clean and was light in weight – much lighter than normal seats yet still safe with a near-15-g rating – well over the 9-g standard rating. The new seat was very comfortable due to having proper cushioning and lower back support that moulded itself to the occupant (all sadly missing from today's ultra-thin seats which promise more leg room but offer less cushion comfort).

A new, advanced, high-volume air-conditioning system and new galley designs transformed the standard of cabin comfort on long flights in hot climates.

The rear-mounted engines meant that the cabin was quieter than any other airliner's – much quieter over the wings than a 707 or DC-8, although after years of service and with worn door seals the VC10 cabin could be a bit noisy right at the back between the engines.

BOAC launched the VC10 with the advertising legend of 'Triumphantly Swift Silent Serene'.

VC10 v 707: Economies of Scale

A fair, later comparison of VC10 figures proved a point:

- B707-420 Conway 508 engines: Range with max payload 4,865 miles/7,830 km.
- Super VC10: Conway 550 engines: Range with max payload 4,720 miles/7,600 km.

Such figures obscured the VC10/Super VC10's superior lifting ability with full or near-full payload at a tropical airfield and to continue en route to destination without an extra refuelling stop.

For the vital VC10/Super VC10 versus Boeing 707 max payload-range battle, a worst case scenario as cited at the time of the mid-1960s, it was suggested that a Standard VC10 after the first year of commercial operations had an average cost per flying hour of £475 alongside a best-case scenario for the (Conway turbofan) 707 at a cost of £371 per flying hour. This difference was so large that many questioned it. Did that figure include the fact that VC10 was achieving notably higher daily hours-in-flight times and much higher load factors? The VC10's costs would come down as experience and daily flying hours built up.

The Super VC10 improved things and BOAC seemed reluctant to reveal their Super VC10 versus 707 economic forensics which at one stage would see the cost of operating the 707 exceed that of the Super VC10. BOAC reported in 1972/73 that its Super VC10s were averaging 11.09 hours

The BOAC tie-up with Cunard was short-lived but gave rise to new titling on the front of the Super VC10, as depicted here.

flying per day against their 707-436s flying much less: 8.7 hours per day. So, the Super VC10s earned more in the air every day. BOAC's full cost figures for revenue flying hours were cited as £486 per hour for the Super VC10 and £510 per hour for the 707-436 – a complete reversal of the so-often-claimed perception of 707's better economy.

An argument was publicly made at the time of the VC10's launch and is still made to this day about payload and range and a sometimes invisible factor – performance and its effect on payload being lifted off the ground. It is true that 707-300 series might lift nearly ten tonnes more, but it could not do it from a hot-and-high airfield with a short runway – a VC10 could, despite the lower total weight of payload: VC10 rarely needed a refuelling stop.

The VC10's heavy-gauge construction added a weight penalty of a suggested 7 tonnes at the aircraft-prepared-for-service (APS) specification in comparison to the more straightforward and lighter-gauge 707 structure (specifically as 707-320B long-range model).

In design terms, there were pros and cons on both sides of the Standard VC10

versus 707-320B airframe argument with many features and issues to consider, but the VC10 scored where it mattered for its intended application in tropical conditions, take-off and flight performance and payload range starting at take-off.

BOAC/BA VC10 and Super VC10 Fleet

Standard VC10 Type 1101

	G-ARVH
G-ARVA	G-ARVI
G-ARVB	G-ARVJ
G-ARVC	G-ARVK
G-ARVE	G-ARVL
G-ARVF	G-ARVM
G-ARVG	
G-ARVG	

Super VC10 Type 1151

	G-ASGJ
G-ASGA	G-ASGK
G-ASGB	G-ASGL
G-ASGC	G-ASGM
G-ASGD	G-ASGN
G-ASGE	G-ASGO
G-ASGF	G-ASGP
G-ASGH	G-ASGR
G-ASGI	

The classic Super VC10 view of BOAC days. Seen with four thrust reversers which were latterly reduced to two to reduce tailplane buffet and resultant fatigue.

Above left: That amazing tail seen from beneath. Engineering as art.

Above right: The complex aerodynamics of the rear engine mounting and Seddon'wing stub seen under the BOAC fin.

Left: The wing root vent supplies the high-volume air-conditioning unit. Note also the details of the inboard wing fence, one of the tallest ever deployed.

Below: Classic BOAC blue in action as the VC10 is captured in the cruise. Note the minimal wing deflection in flight, due to the stiff wing.

Top: G-ASGR poses for the British Airways cameraman. BOAC morphed into British Airways from late 1974 in a mix and match of hybrid liveries. Despite losing the Speedbird emblem on the fin, the Super VC10 looked good in the 'BA' red, white and blue scheme – remaining in service with the airline until 1981.

Above: BOAC Super VC10 G-ASGB in the defining BOAC golden speedbird'livery depicted climbing hard out of Africa in the 1970s. From an aviation painting by Lance Cole.

Left: The later BOAC/British Airways interior refit as applied to the Super VC10 fleet, and as seen in the First Class section. Sadly, in-flight entertainment was lacking. People could always read a book.

BOAC in-flight and handling differences

Flight crew training took place principally out of Shannon, Ireland, Prestwick Scotland and London Heathrow, but it was amid the gusty Atlantic winds of south west Eire that the new VC10 crews learned their trade. They were ably taught by a cadre of highly experience pilots, many of which had wartime experience and Comet jetliner flying experience. Ex-RAF wartime pilot and Comet training Captain Tom Stoney was arguably the lead figure in teaching older men and young recruits how to handle the massive beast.

Of significance, the Standard VC10 and the Super VC10 would, despite their dimensional differences, be commonly rated for flying licence terms. If you were licensed to fly one, you were automatically licensed to fly the other – after a short conversion course.

The Super VC10 was longer and needed a different technique when turning on tight taxiways and runways, being steered further into the available hard surface before turning in order the to allow the rear, and the main undercarriage room to follow-through without cutting onto the grass.

Interestingly and often ignored, Super VC10 had an additional flap setting to assist take-off performance. The was a 14.5-degree flap setting that provide sufficient lift but less drag than the 20-degree flap setting that was normal for the Standard VC10. Because the Super VC10 operated in less extreme temperatures from more 'normal' runways, it could have a longer take-off run and a less critical take-off flap setting. However, SuperVC10 retained the ability to be deployed on tropical routes and use the 20-degree flap, take-off performance parameters.

The Super VC10 had very slightly different characteristics at the stall, at high weight/high altitude, and during 'Dutch Roll' flight behaviour recovery. Super VC10 added a few knots to its landing sped if heavily laden and was more likely to catch a cross wind due to its greater fuselage side area. Of course with the uprated Rolls-Royce Conway 550 engines, it had more power, yet it weighed more than a Standard, not least from being bigger and having 1,250 gallons of fuel carried in the wet tailfin with its integral fuel tank. The longer forward cabin with more structural weight and more passenger weight, reduced the c.g. – centre-of-gravity – effects of having a heavier tail aft of the centre-of-gravity.

Such differences in Super VC10 handling were also due to its revised wing aerofoil, longer engine–mounting stub wings, and differing fuselage length. Yet the handling and performance differences were small enough for the two different VC10 variations to be rated by the authorities as close enough to be dual-type rated and licensed for pilots.

The BOAC Standard VC10 lacked the revised wingtips of later Standards and the Supers did not have these wingtips either. There were also configuration changes to outboard wing fences across the Standard Type 1101-1103 VC10s with the Type 1101 full chord fence changed.

After the Type 1100 prototype G-ARTA had made its maiden flight (without the tall in-board wing fence) on 29 June 1962, the low-percentage cruise drag rise problems were noticed. The solutions or fixes were to change the engine and exhaust profiles and add the curved Kuchemann (of D. Kuchemann the RAE aerodynamicist) wingtips which slightly increased the wing area from the so-called V1100 small-wing. Thus G-ARTA the VC10 prototype's wingspan was 140 feet 2 inches (42.7 metres), while the production Type 1101 and series airframes featured a wing change to 146 feet 2 inches (44.55 metres). Civil airworthiness certification was achieved on 23 April 1964, and BOAC introduced the Type 1101 VC10 into service on its London–Lagos route just a week later – in an early gold-edged cheatline livery, with Captain Rendall at the helm; Captain Stoney flew the return flight.

Of interest, the first Super VC10 proving flight across the Atlantic on 7 March 1965 (commanded by Captain N. Todd) with BOAC flight test airframe G-ASGD, landed in New York after 6 hours and 54 minutes, with a significant figure of over 3 hours of fuel (just under 20,000kgs) remaining in the tanks (despite air traffic control restrictions on route from London Heathrow, with resultant height and speed/Mach number constraints). This excess fuel, despite headwinds and air traffic issues, demonstrated the Super VC10s, payload-range and fuel consumption using stepped climb procedures and in-flight trimming.

The early Standard VC10 prototype G-ARTA seen in pre-delivery, early BOAC markings during 1960s flight testing over England. From an aviation painting by Lance Cole.

Technical Specifications:
(1) Standard VC10 Type 1101 (12 built for BOAC)
(2) Super VC10 Type 1151-1154 (17 built for BOAC: 5 built for EAA)
Note* Type 1102/1103 for GH and BUA have differences to Type 1101 baseline model

Construction
Reinforced, double-bubble semi-monocoque fuselage and wings built in steel, aluminium, hidmium, titanium, copper, zinc and other metals and alloys. Major parts and panels integrally machined from solid metal billets. Major panels constructed in large one-piece torsionally rigid panels. Significant fuselage, wingbox and tailfin reinforcing structures. Four-shear web triple torsion box at wing. Over-sized fuselage frames, hoops and cleats. Reduced use of rivets and extensive use of advanced bonding and anti-corrosion measures

Powerplants
(1) Standard VC10: 4 x 21,000-lb (94.1 kN) thrust Rolls-Royce Conway 42/540 turbofans
(2) Super VC10: 4 x 22,500-lb (100.1 kN) thrust Rolls-Royce Conway 43/550B turbofans
Max wing loading of Super VC10 (2) at max take-off weight: 12,278 lb/sq ft (5,581 kg/m²)
Max wing loading of Super VC10 (2) at max landing weight: 80.8 lb/sq ft (394.5 kg/m²)

Dimensions
Wing span
(1) 146 ft 2in (44.55 m)
(2) 146 ft 2in (44.55 m)
Length
(1) 158 ft 8in (48.36 m)
(2) 171 ft 8in (52.32 m)
Height
(1) 39 ft 6 in (12.04 m)
(2) 39 ft 6 in (12.04 m)
Wing area
(1) 2,851 ft² (264.8 m²)
(2) 2,932 ft² (272.4 m²)
Aspect ratio
(1) 7.5
(2) 7.3
Sweep at 1/4 chord
32.5 degrees
Tailplane span
43 ft 10 in (13.36 m)
Tailplane area
638 ft² (59.3 m²)
Wheelbase
(1) 65 ft 11 in (20.09 m)
(2) 72 ft 1.5 in (21.98 m)
Wheel track
21 ft 5 in (6.53 m)
Fuselage width (external)
12 ft 4 in (3.76 m)
Fuselage height (external)
14 ft 1.5 in (4.31 m)
Fuel capacity
(1) 17,925 gal (81,487 l) in wing and centre section tanks
(2) 19,340 gal (87,920 l) in wing, centre section and fin tanks
Accommodation
(1) 135/139 passengers in two classes and configurations. 150+ in single class high density

(2) 151 in two classes. Mixed seating/ratio combi option. Maximum 163 passengers six abreast in full pax configuration
Cabin dimensions
Length (1): 92 ft 4 in (28.14 m)
Length (2): 105 ft (32.00 m)
Width: 11 ft 6 in (3.50 m)
Height: 7 ft 5 in (2.26 m)
Weights
Basic operating empty
(1) 146,980 lb (66,670 kg)
(2) 156,828 lb (71,137 kg)
Max take-off
(1) 312,000 lb (141,523 kg)
(2) 335,000 lb (151,953 kg)
Max zero fuel
(1) 187,400 lb (85,004 kg)
(2) 215,000 lb (97,524 kg)
Max landing
(1) 216,000 lb (97,978 kg)
(2) 237,000 lb (107,503 kg)
Max payload:
(1) 40,420 lb (18,335 kg)
(2) 58,172 lb (26,369 kg)
Performance
Max cruise
Max cruise of 580 mph (933.42 km/h) still air (higher speed possible with tailwind)
520 kts (950 km/h) at 25,000 ft
505 kts (935 km/h) at 31,000 ft
Economical cruise
(1) Best cost: 480 kts (890 km/h) at 25,000 ft
Long range: 369 kts (684 km/h) at 30,000 ft
Long range/high speed: 476 kts (882 km/h) at 38,000 ft
(2) Best cost: 478 kts (885 km/h) at 34,000 ft
Long range: 476 kts (882 km/h) at 38,000 ft
Long range/high speed: 505 kts (936 km/h) at 31,000 ft
Performance above 40,000 ft type dependent: Ref Type 1102/1103
Typical, minimum, final landing approach speeds at known max load landing weight value and nil crosswind:
(1) 135 kts (251 km/h)
(2) 137 kts (255 km/h)
Design limit speeds
Mach 0.86, VC 303 kts (562 km/h) EAS
Mach 0.94 VD 379 kts (702 km/h) EAS
Operational ceiling
(1) Type 1101: 38,000 ft (11,582 m)
Note* Type 1102/3: 43,000 ft (13,106 m)
(2) Type 1151–1154: 38,000 ft (11,582 m)
Max payload range (no reserves)
(1) 4,380 nm (8,112 km)
(2) 4,100 nm (7,600 km)
Max fuel range (no reserves)
(1) 5,275 nm (9,765 km)
(2) 6,195 nm (11,473 km)
Flying controls
Fully powered, artificial feel, four hydraulic fail-safe systems. All primary surfaces have separate sections each powered by separate electro-hydraulic power units. Variable incidence tailplane. Stick-pusher fitted. Super VC10 with additional 14-degree flap setting for improved take-off performance. Autopilot and Autoland system fitted.

RAF Service: Transport to Tanker

RAF Transport Command, or post-1967 as Support Command, was in fact the RAF's own de facto airline and as the jet age changed amid the military aviation fighters and bombers of the era, the RAF needed a large and fast transport aircraft to supply and service the materials and men such machines demanded.

Just as was the case for BOAC, Comet 4 was too small and the Britannia – however brilliant – too slow and too small but nevertheless, enduringly useful. The fact was however, that uniquely, a fleet of RAF No. 10 Squadron VC10s could, in one go, rapidly deliver for deployment, over 500 troops (armed infantry), a mix of men and freight including armour, to 14 tonnes weight (with bombs and vehicles in the cargo hold). It could fly non-stop nearly 4,000 miles away (or further with in-flight refuelling) in well under one day. Alternatively, an RAF VC10 could rescue a large number of casualties with 76 stretcher casevac cases and an on-board medical set-up with operating facility. It was natural then that the VC10 project should include an RAF variant from the start. Indeed, Sir George Edwards cited the RAF as the VC10's most nationally important user. In

the record of VC10 and BOAC history we cannot ignore the RAF VC10 story – not least as BOAC shared with the RAF some aspects of VC10 crew training and down-the-line maintenance.

The RAF's C.Mk.1 VC10s were tweaked airframes and the original variants were hot-rods of the air because they had the more powerful Conway engines from the Super VC10 and the revised wing of the developed Super VC10 – itself stemming from work on the aerodynamics of the VC10's wing first seen on the Type 1102 VC10 airframes. With the forward cargo door added and a stronger cabin floor designed to take cargo loads using a roller movement system, the RAF VC10s were heavier and more powerful. The RAF VC10 remit was thus less focused on seat-per-mile costs and long-range operating economics, and more on range-to-payload and mixed cabin configuration abilities.

At maximum weight, the heavier and more fuel-thirsty VC10 C.Mk.1 had a shorter max-payload range than a Standard-model VC10 – 3,185 nm, but a higher 59,000-lb payload which might include vehicles in the cargo cabin. However, provided it was not heavily loaded up to MTOW, an RAF

XV106, a 1966-built original white and blue RAF VC10 latterly converted to Type C.Mk.1K, shows off the in-flight refuelling probe as it taxies gently along the tarmac.

Left: RAF VC10 grabs at the sky in a near 20-degree climb at full power after using less than 1,800 feet of runway at Kemble. Empty and light, she almost glided the eight-minute-flight back to Brize Norton.

Below: This shot captures the angle of the nose and forward fuselage roof contours at an angle rarely obvious. The RAF kept their VC10s spick and span right to the end – in September 2013.

VC10 C.Mk.1 with a lighter load, could, with high altitude cruise levels, achieve a range of 5,000 miles. This despite extra weight: even the seats (rearward facing) in the RAF VC10 were heavier.

Numerous other production changes included an auxiliary power unit, a standard fit hydraulic ram air turbine (HYRAT) emergency hydraulic generator to complement the electrical ram air turbine (ELRAT). These differences created the distinct RAF VC10 C.Mk.1 – or Vickers Type 1106.

Vickers had received its RAF VC10 orders in September 1961 – for an initial five airframes and the team set to work to create the RAF specification VC10. A total of 14 RAF VC10s were ordered but the fleet was reduced by one airframe that went to the Rolls-Royce fleet as a test bed for the RB211 high-bypass ratio development testing programme as G-AXLR. But it was not until Christmas of 1965 that the first RAF VC10 took its test flight – just over a year after the first civil-specification BOAC VC10 entered service.

RAF VC10 Design Development

The key for the original C.Mk.1 design developments was in wing, engine and structural changes. Of note, fitment of the forward fuselage cargo door and its mechanism added weight and a very small local aerodynamic penalty around its frame.

The stronger floor which could take a load of 1,000 lb/ft^2 added weight which allowed a near-6,000-lb maximum load with spreaders – more than enough for a vehicle or bomb rack.

The Super VC10 engines – the Conway 550s – had by this time been uprated from 22,500-lb to 22,800-lb thrust as a 550B by inserting an extra intermediate compressor stage and which were added to the RAF VC10s.

A definite RAF-specific option was a self-starter for the VC10 – ideal in non-airline locations, by the addition of the Bristol Siddeley Artouste auxiliary power unit (APU) and the revised tail cone to house it. The sheet metal at the nose was altered too – to allow provision for the addition of an in-flight refuelling probe.

Various minor fuselage and floor reinforcements, internal trims and furnishing changes and, of course, the heavy, extra-comfort 'tombstone'-backed passenger seats catered for large physical frames and all such seats were rear-facing for safety (to absorb G-force in an impact).

Flight deck instrumentation and specifications included military options and devices/updates which in later years would see the RAF VC10 fleet fitted with more advanced ground-proximity warning system and, of note, the TCAS anti-terrain-and-airborne-collision warning system.

Transport Command VC10s

The last of the RAF's new VC10s was XV109 which was delivered as late as 1 August 1968 (retired 6 April 2010). Painted in the all-white RAF livery with a bright blue cheatline Z-flash, the No. 10 Squadron RAF VC10s looked very different indeed to the BOAC versions. BOAC's cancelled Super VC10 orders meant that the RAF could jump in and get quicker VC10 C.Mk.1 build slots for its airframes. The first RAF VC10 registered as XR806 took off from the Brooklands short runway on 26 November 1965, entering RAF service with the reformed No. 10 Squadron in July 1966 but not performing its first full RAF airline Transport Command duties until early 1967 after months of crew training and route proving all over the world, where,

on occasion, local BOAC VC10 knowledge came to assist.

The homebase for the RAF VC10 years was Brize Norton in Oxfordshire. Its single runway saw continuous VC10 operations up to late September 2013 and with some poignancy saw the ex-BOAC/BA, Gulf Air and EAA civil airframes return to service from a base deep in the English countryside.

From 1966 RAF Transport/Support Command received its own distinct VC10 and used them to build the RAF's equivalent of a daily, worldwide air transport service. With room for 150 troops, or a lower seat number of 139 in airline-standard comfort, or a mixed load of cargo or medical/casualty evacuation accommodation, the fleet (all named after RAF Victoria Cross holders) began the legend of the VC10 in RAF service. At its 1970s height the RAF's own airline at Brize Norton carried nearly 10,000 passengers a month and operated

On the command deck, RAF tanker during refuelling exercise. Note the addition of digital electronic flight deck displays and kit including TCAS. In-flight refuelling was not without risk.

Gear up! As the undercarriage doors accept the main gear, this RAF VC10 with wing-mounted refuelling pods grabs at the sky as the Conways smoke. The large area of the trailing, Fowler-type flaps is clearly seen in this view of an unusual 'Flaps 20' take-off.

an airline-style check-in facility. Some of the VC10 fleet were averaging 200 flying hours a month. Daily or several-times-weekly services to Aden, Cyprus, Gan, Germany, Hong Kong, Singapore and Washington, all ran with a VC10 precision.

Inside the RAF's massive VC10 base hangar, were carried out the repairs and maintenance of the RAF fleet with up to six VC10s being accommodated at the same time inside the building – where the RAF also experienced an unfortunate VC10 jacking accident as had BOAC, BUA and EAA.

Royal/VIP VC10

A principal role for the RAF VC10 fleet had been royal and VIP/diplomatic flights all over the world for over 30 years. The first use of the VC10 was in May 1965 when Her Majesty the Queen visited Ethiopia by BOAC VC10. RAF C.Mk.1s for Royal or VIP duties could be converted into a VIP cabin arrangement with tables, sofas and beds.

We should note that like BOAC, the RAF never lost a VC10. This speaks volumes for the quality of design and pilot training and behaviours of both organizations.

The RAF C.Mk.1 VC10 fleet achieved excellent reliability figures and where problems arose the RAF developed its own techniques for solving them – in fact it implemented a schedule of preventative rather than reactive measures. This included coming up with a new, quicker and cheaper way of changing the tailplane by chemically freezing and shrinking the main mounting pivot and inserting it cold, thus ensuring a lower stress level during fitting.

As in airline service, VC10 could develop problems with axles and brakes; the RAF experienced several such events. A fleet-wide axle replacement programme stemmed from an incident of axle failure. The RAF's high utilization rates revealed a need for a different grade of engine oil and a limitation on nose wheel tyre degradations due to the dangers of the engines ingesting thrown tyre

treads. The RAF VC10 maintenance team at Brize Norton developed a VC10-specific, travelling spares package of vital items which could be accommodated in the main hold. This ensured that en-route issues could be dealt with rather than having to wait for spares. Just as with BOAC service, the lack of many other operators en route meant that the VC10 had to look after itself.

No. 10 Squadron was to be disbanded in late 2005, the remaining C.Mk.1s transferred over to 101 Squadron and latterly reconfigured.

VC10 K.MK.2, K.MK.3 & K.MK.4
Later RAF Airframe Conversions

In 1981, BOAC's successor, British Airways, placed its just-retired fleet of Super VC10s in a field at Abingdon, Oxfordshire – and at Prestwick, Scotland – where they would be stored for many weather-worn years, in some cases badly rotting away, along with the remaining early BOAC Standard VC10 airframes to be disposed of.

It was the ex-Gulf Air fleet of BOAC Standards ferried to Bristol Filton that inspired an idea – rebuilding VC10 airliners as RAF air-to-air flight refuelling tankers as formulated by the government in 1978 under ASR 406 schedule.

Next up would come the four remaining East African Airways Super VC10s – the last machines built including the 1970 airframe: the EAA Super VC10s had been repossessed in 1977 and were still relatively fresh in age but had endured more short-flight cycles.

The 1981-withdrawn BA Super VC10 fleet were assessed and six had to be scrapped due to very high hours and corrosion after nearly twenty years of service and over five years' storage in damp conditions at Abingdon. Others (five) were salvageable and they would form the fleet of five K.Mk.4 RAF machines registered as ZD235 to ZD240.

After years in damp, external storage, wrapped in sweating plastic and then

One RAF VC10 C1 airframe was used to test the new Rolls-Royce RB211 high-by-pass fan jet (for Boeing 747 and Lockheed Tristar installation) on one side of the VC10 G-AXLR only. This created significant torsional airframe forces, leading after the test programme to the grounding of the aircraft. Fitting one such RB211 to each side of the VC10 was considered as a production project to re-engine the VC10 for greater fuel economy.

coated in oil, the ex-BOAC/BA Super VC10 fleet from Abingdon were in poor condition and had to be flown over to Filton with their flaps, slats and gear locked down in a series of flights that represented some risk. Much expense was required to deal with the effects of years of static storage in British weather. This included new skins to the top of the structurally vital, centre wing torsion box – a very complicated job.

The conversion of these ex-BA airframes did not include any fuel tanks being inserted into the fuselages, instead relying on the original aircraft's wing, body and fin fuel tanks to supply an air-to-air refuelling ability. The first of these conversions – to Type K.Mk.4 – was to be ZD242 (ex G-ASGP) which first flew on 20 July 1993 but was not in RAF service until April 1994.

The RAF's original fleet of C.Mk.1 VC10s were also subjected to a multi-million-pound refurbishment programme (carried out by BAE/FR Aviation Hurn) which extended their lives and added the refuelling capability, but with just two underwing refuelling pods. They lost their all-white livery and emerged in the grey/blue hue that became the later-life RAF VC10 standard. The refurbished C.Mk.1s became C1.K types.

The K.2 label applied to the ex-BOAC/Gulf Air machines as a new Type number of 1112, and the K.3 name applied to the ex-EAA Super VC10s as Type 1164. The whole rebuilding project was ordered via the Weybridge-Bristol Division of British Aerospace (latterly BAE). K.4 applied to the ex-BA machines. K.2 carried 85 tons of fuel, K.3 carried 90 tons

A principal tanker fleet upgrade was the fitting of the developed Conway 550B engine with 22,800-lb static thrust across all the

airframes at some expense. Each wing had a flight refuelling pod with a 50-foot trailing hose and localized reinforcement of the outer wing was required for the mounting points. A third, central drum-type HDU 81-foot-hose refuelling point was applied under the tail of the K.Mk.2 that required revised metalwork to the lower fuselage lobe. The extra fuel tankage was applied inside the old passenger cabin and featured five double-skinned, cylindrical metal tanks on bearer frames, with flexible membrane cells in each tank. Fitting a nose-mounted flight refuelling probe also added to the range of the tanker itself – offering good flexibility wherever the deployment. Only the oil capacity of each engine could be the limiting endurance factor.

A whole new array of electronic systems for control, navigation and communications (including TCAS) were added to the old analogue-clockwork VC10 flight decks. CCTV would be fitted to enable the fuel operator to closely monitor the receiving aircraft.

The ex-BOAC/Gulf Air Standard variant machines had had to have holes cut in their roof panels to insert the tanks – but the ex-EAA machines were equipped with the cabin cargo door, making conversion easier and cheaper in terms of metal and man hours.

For safe conversion and a new 'zero-timed' parts replacement programme to be effective, the VC10s and Super VC10s were stripped bare down to their keels, cleats, and under-skin structures. Everything was forensically examined, microscopically sampled and replaced or repaired where necessary. From fin supports to wing ribs and wing boxes, from engine struts to tailplane skins, to windows, the airframes

Conversion at Filton. ZD242 gets stripped back to bare metal after years of airline service during the tanker conversion process.

The ex-BUA/BCAL G-ATDJ then served as XX914 with the RAF at Bedford only to end its life as a scrapper but with a fuselage section sent to Brize Norton for training use.

were effectively remanufactured – at least there were plenty of spares lying about.

The first K.Mk.2 was ZA141 (ex-G-ARVG) that first flew as a tanker on 22 June 1982, wearing a camouflage livery not common to subsequent airframes; the first K.Mk.3 was to be ZA148 (ex-5Y-ADA) and first flown as a tanker on 3 July 1984. Hemp, grey, and blue/grey became the alter RAF K-series liveries.

The K.Mk.1–K.Mk.4 conversion project, despite cost overruns resulting from unforeseen works and delays, the idea and the outcome were a great success and added over a decade to the VC10's life. The cost overrun resulted not from bad project management, but from an alleged pre-project initial underestimate of the work required to the VC10s that had been stored, and the costs and time required – so found a Parliamentary Select Committee that looked at the issue of the bill for £130 million.

The RAF reformed an original ex-Royal Flying Corps bomber squadron as 101 Squadron – to create a VC10/Super VC10 tanker fleet nucleus at Brize Norton – initially termed as a Tanker Training Flight – the TTF. 101 Squadron had last operated the mighty Vulcan in 1982 and been disbanded the same year. Officially reforming on 1 May 1984, the squadron existed alongside 10 Squadron at Brize Norton and made the most of that squadron's three decades of VC10 operational and maintenance expertise.

With its high T-tail, stable flight characteristics and smooth handling, the VC10 proved a popular in-flight refuelling tanker as it allowed manoeuvring receiving pilots more room to move and less danger of collision with a low-set tailplane as found on other tanker types. There were also no exhaust streams or buffeting from wing-mounted engines to contend with for pilots flying close up behind and below the VC10's wing-mounted and under-fuselage refuelling hoses. This was a major plus for reliable refuelling. However, for the VC10 to refuel from another VC10, care had to be taken as the receiver's tailplane and fin could be buffeted by exhaust and airflow from the donating VC10 – the receiver's high T-tail being in-line and at nearly the same height with the four Conways of the mother ship.

Across the Gulf wars (Iraq), Afghan, Libyan and other conflicts alongside normal global military deployments, the RAF tanker fleet has racked up an envious, accident-free record of service to a number of other air forces as well as to RAF types. The RAF VC10s provided over 25 percent of the in-flight refuelling for the US Navy during the original Gulf conflict. Of interest, 101 Squadron has performed a number of VC10-to-VC10 in-flight refuellings that have allowed events such as flying from the UK (Brize Norton) to Perth, Australia, with just two in-flight refuelling sessions across a 9,000-mile non-stop route on a 15 hour 53-minute flight with ex-EAA machine 5H-MMT as RAF ZA147. It would be 2019 before Qantas made such a non-stop flight a commercial, passenger-carrying reality with a Boeing 787.

The weekly VC10 service to the Falkland Islands also provided numerous challenges to the RAF crews, and again, no major incident, nor accident ever occurred. Ex-EAA 5H-MMT as ZA147 also flew the last RAF flight back from the Falklands RAF Mount Pleasant and made the last operational VC10 sortie to be the last VC10 to land at Brize Norton. ZA147 was the last VC10 to make an air show appearance. ZA147 then headed to Bruntingthorpe where it remains an exhibit.

Far from providing over a decade's planned service up to 2000 as planned, the RAF VC10 fleet flew on until nearly 2014. By this time however, the costs of keeping the Conways maintained and fuelled, and of addressing the fatigue issues of these very-hard worked airframes with their flight cycles beyond original design life, had become prohibitive. Major expenses such as wing-skin and fuselage panel and structural section replacement have, quite expectedly, had to be performed.

Above: The RAF's first all-white VC10 C.Mk.1 XR806 seen on first flight in 1965.

Left: The RAF's XR808 with 101 Squadron's anniversary markings in 2012 at RAF Fairford during the last days of the type's operations service with RAF. Note the generous wing area and revised wingtip design.

No. 10 Squadron operated its VC10s for an astonishing 39 years.

RAF VC10 Finale

After years of RAF service amid 50 years of RAF association, the VC10 made its final air-to-air refuelling operational sortie on 20 September 2013, and retired from service on 25 September 2013. Two VC10s, ZA147 and ZA150, flew together in a sortie that involved refuelling one VC10 from the other. The VC10 officially had its last flight on 25 September, before landing at Bruntingthorpe airfield at 1602 hours after two very noisy go-arounds, when ZA147 (ex-EAA's 5H-MMT) shut the log book on 47 years of RAF service and 51.3 years of total VC10 flight.

RAF VC10 details:
- RAF VC10 C.Mk.1 Type 1106
- XR806 *George Thompson VC*
- XR807 *Donald Garland VC/Thomas Gray VC*
- XR808 *Kenneth Campbell VC*
- XR809 to Rolls-Royce as G-AXLR for RB.211 trials with one engine only. Scrapped due to alleged distorted airframe from asymmetric thrust loading from test engine.
- XR810 *David Lord VC*

- XV101 *Lanoe Hawker VC*
- XV102 *Guy Gibson VC*
- XV103 *Edward Mannock VC*
- XV104 *James McCudden VC*
- XV105 *Albert Ball VC*
- XV106 *Thomas Mottershead VC*
- XV107 *James Nicholson VC*
- XV108 *William Rhodes-Moorhouse VC*
- XV109 *Arthur Scarf VC*
- RAF VC10 K.Mk.2 as Type 1112
- ZA140 ex A40-VL
- ZA141 ex-A40-VG
- ZA142 ex-A40-VI
- ZA143 ex-A40-VK
- ZA144 ex-A40-VC
- RAF VC10 K.Mk.3 as Type 1164
- ZA147 ex-5H-MMT
- ZA148 ex-5Y-ADA
- ZA149 ex-5X-UVJ
- ZA150 ex-5H-MOG
- RAF VC10 K.Mk.4 as Type 1170
- ZD230 ex-G-ASGA
- ZD235 ex-G-ASGG
- ZD240 ex-G-ASGL
- ZD241 ex-G-ASGM
- ZD242 ex-G-ASGP

Note* other ZD airframes registered but not converted (scrapped).

Note** Victoria Cross (VC) markings were altered/swapped as airframes were retired.

The original RAF airframes had uprated Conways compared to the BOAC/BUA/and other Standard Types, and a rate of climb of over 1,000 feet per minute more than a Standard BOAC series VC10. Add in the cargo door, bigger wing and stronger floor, and the RAF had an adaptable airframe that lasted into conversion to tanker capability. Latterly the final Conway 550B upgraded engines from the late-model Supers would go into the RAF fleet.

During the later conversions of the RAF C Types and the ex-airline machines, the main work was the fitting of in-flight refuelling equipment, tankage and reinforcements to the structure and deletion of some windows. The Flight Refuelling Mk.28 HDU was seen under each wing and actually provided some new, wing-bending relief and only minimal drag.

A Flight Refuelling Mark 17B HDU was fitted on the rear fuselage centreline (but not on all conversions).

The RAF spec flight deck saw added fuelling system operator controls, closed-circuit TV system, and night-vision lighting for the refuelling system. An in-flight refuelling probe was fitted to the nose with associated plumbing routings to the tanks.

Extra tankage included five 940gallon fuel drums in the fuselage, mounted on bearers – but not in the old BOAC/BA Supers VC10s.

The airframe and other systems were generally refurbished, with structural reinforcements added where necessary, notably at wing box, tail support, wing plating and windows.

The uprated Conway 550 engines were added to the ex-BOAC/BA/Gulf Air machines as the K2 series.

RAF VC10 Type History at 10 Squadron and 101 Squadron

VC10 C1: RAF VC10 Type 1106
14 Built with 13 original C1 converted to VC10 C1K.
VC10 C1K: RAF VC10 Type 1180
Converted from VC10 C1, 2-point HDU refuelling and no fuselage cabin deck tanks.
VC10 K2: RAF VC10 Type 1112
5 Conversions to inflight refuelling from Type 1101 BOAC/BA/Gulf Air airframes.
VC10 K3: RAF VC10 Type 1164
4 Conversions to inflight refuelling from Type 1154, with 3-point HDU refuelling and fuselage/cabin tanks in these ex-EAA airframes.
VC10 K4: RAF VC10 Type 1170
5 Conversions to inflight-refuelling from Type 1151, 3-point refuelling but no fuselage/cabin tanks in these ex-BOAC/BA airframes.

Further RAF VC10 types were suggested in the early 1960s but never built as then specified (but a converted-tanker version was latterly conceived). These earlier military design projects included:
- Air-launched ballistic missile carrier
- Maritime reconnaissance airframe
- Bomber
- Multi-Role
- Tanker

Left: RAF in-flight refuelling from a converted ex-East African Airways Super VC10. A Harrier takes fuel from the RAF tanker. The Rolls-Royce Conway 550s are churning away at high altitude.

Right: VC10 K2 tanker registred ZA141 was the first conversion to fly and the only one to take to the air in the camouflage livery. Here it is captured in the moment of lift-off from Filton after conversion.

RAF VC10s – high lift hot rods and tanker tens

The RAF learned many tricks and tweaks to increase the efficiency and life-span of its VC10 operations. A fact sometimes obscured is that just like BOAC, the RAF had its own people based at Vickers during the design and development of its specific VC10 Type 1106 in order to maximise the potential of the new airframe and the upgrades that came through from the VC10 and Super VC10 development process of 1963–1965.

To service its 'shiny new tens' as the RAF called them, the RAF built a major new hangar at its VC10 base – RAF Brize Norton where it could service its VC10 fleet from the reformed No. 10 Squadron that was Oxfordshire based from 1966. Known as Base Hangar, this massive new structure could house five VC10s inside with ease, more at a push. From this base came the expert maintenance and fettling that kept the RAF VC10 fleet in its major transport uplift status as a global player for four decades. RAF St Athan would latterly be a further base unit for the converted RAF VC10 fleet of tankers and mixed ability VC10 airframes.

Brize Norton housed the VC10 operational conversion unit (OCU). Early RAF operations also saw new RAF VC10 crews spend some time riding on the cockpits (flightdecks) of BOAC VC10s on live route sectors in order to gain a real appreciation of VC10 flying requirements and handling techniques. The RAF did not initially have a VC10 simulator so used the BOAC simulators at Cranebank-Heathrow. Latterly the RAF received a suite of VC10 simulators.

VC10 deployments to strategic exercises and conflict zones meant that the VC10 fleet had to be independent and able to look after itself anywhere in the world and not just at RAF outstations.

The RAF's earlier C1 or C Mk.1 fleet were of course technical hybrids with the Super VC10 wings, engine mountings, uprated Conways to an initial thrust boost, then latterly to equal the Super VC10 Conway 550B specification. With the cargo door and strengthened floor with its roller load and pallet movement function, the fleet were very versatile and carried many differing loads. Spare engines could be accommodated in the cabin if their weight was correctly spread, so the RAF made less use of the airline-spec VC10's 'fifth' engine-carrying pod that could be fitted under the wing to transport a spare engine (in an aerodynamically faired pod).

Further adaptability in the RAF fleet came in the form of the Royal or VIP interior kit (sometimes adapted for on certain BOAC Royal flight configurations). Special chairs, tables, and staff seating were able to be installed (in a forward to mid-fuselage location) quite quickly, although hard-used RAF VC10 cabins might have needed a clean before the VIP guests boarded. Several days were needed to prepare a Royal/VIP Government flight VC10. After HRH Queen

Last days of the VC10. On finals, the classic view of the VC10, this time a later RAF C1K conversion and displaying generous slat and flap at approach speed of under 140 knots. Note the in-flight refuelling probe in place.

Elizabeth II, the most famous users of the RAF VC10 on the international stage had to be various British Prime Ministers, notably M. H. Thatcher.

The RAF ran its own in-house airline from Brize Norton and the VC10 fleet made daily or weekly scheduled departures from an airline-style terminal. Daily flights to the USA and down to the tropical outstations of the old empire network (Cyprus, Singapore, Hong Kong, Gan, and to Africa) and it ran like clockwork from Brize Norton in a massive logistical exercise employing thousands of people. The post-1982 Falklands situation and the need for a fulltime flight corridor from Britain to the South Atlantic outpost added flight cycles and hours to the RAF VC10 airframes.

The RAF VC10 crews did not just include the flying crew: also vital were the loadmasters and on-board cabin crew members who looked after the cargo, passengers and medial/casevac stretcher cases on long haul routes. The entire VC10 cabin could be turned into a mobile hospital and stretcher –racked casualty station offering room for 78 stretcher cases and normal seating for walking wounded and medical crew.

Although RAF VC10s could in case of serious issue make use of BOAC VC10 spares network out on the worldwide route network, the RAF's own routes obviously differed from BOAC's and despite having VC10 spares strategically located down the line, each RAF VC10 had to carry its own vital package of spares despite the payload

Doing a touch and go at Kemble, the C1K captured in the perfect VC10 pose of nose up, flaps down, tail set, and the lightest of touchdowns into wind on the main gear at about 130 knots, which is 20 knots or more slower than the competing airframes could manage.

considerations of such. The pack included spare tyres, wheels, brake fittings, fuel systems fittings, electronics items, pipes, lines, strappings, undercarriage parts, and a general engine maintenance spare parts inventory. The infamous silver duct tape was not ignored as a temporary repair patch mechanism, even by the RAF VC10 men.

The RAF pioneered new maintenance techniques at Brize Norton for the VC10 fleet and this included a quicker way (via chemical/temperature/metallurgical effect) of demounting/remounting the vital tailplane and its pivot and screw-jack.

101 Squadron and its VC10 operations latterly came to the fore of VC10 in the Air-to-Air Refuelling (AAR) flight refuelling operations. An in-flight aerial refuelling tanker school was established at Brize Norton and an operational conversion unit or OCU was part of this tanker training facility. 101 Squadron took to the air with its VC10 tanker conversion fleet via the K2 and K3 fleets. The K2 was active in service from 1984, the K3 went operational in 1985, and 101 Squadron received its first ex-BA Super VC10 as a K4 as late as July 1993.

The VC10's safety and ease of in-flight refuelling for smaller aircraft came from the VC10's T-tail design and resulting extra clearance and smoother air behind the dispensing tanker. The lack of wing-mounted engines and their exhaust plumes (as seen in the 707-Type KC135 tanker) also meant smoother flying under and behind the VC10 in comparison to that main rival.

RAF VC10 developments included the use of a special aileron float technique which reduced stress/fatigue on the then-ageing VC10s wing spars and structures by reducing bending loads upon the wing from lifting forces by adding aileron up (by set degrees between 2 degrees and 6 degrees, according to aircraft weight in-flight) to induce localised lift loss over the wingtips and therefore reduce bending forces and stresses.

Of particular interest in terms of wing stresses and ongoing updates, the VC10 tanker conversion also saw the addition of saw-tooth localized flow/vortex-generator fences to the wings of certain K-series types.

Of note is that the K3 and K4 wings (fitted with outer-section HDU units) can show more flex and dihedral than previously seen on an in-flight civilian series Super VC10, notably during manoeuvres. The original VC10 series was noted for its stiff wing and lack of notable dihedral in-flight. Later in their lives, circa 2012, wing fatigue issues saw limitations put upon the numbers of crew and passengers allowed to fly on these airframes. This was no reflection upon the VC10 design, but a reflection on what the aircraft had been asked to do over five decades of expected and unexpected use.

The RAF K4 fleet, the ex-BA Super VC10s, did not have internal cabin fuel cells added as part of their conversion and thus used their own long range capability to refuel external receivers and to fly themselves, all from the same on-board source. However, they were not as structurally fresh as the ex-EAA machines used for the K3 airframes and it was 1994 before a K4 was fully in-service with the RAF after much rebuilding and refreshing of the airframe had taken place.

The RAF C1 fleet and the later 'tanker tens' became as famous and as loved as the civilian airline chapters of the VC10 and Super VC10 history. Only fate, finance and politics stopped the further development of the military variations and developments of the VC10 airframe. Anti-Ballistic Missile Bombers, Maritime (rescue/reconnaissance) types, Multi-Role extended range tankers with 6,500-mile range, all were considered, planned and drawn up by Vickers designers (inside BAC). A three-fuselage, all-wing type VC10 transport was drawn up in 1964 and envisaged six Rolls-Royce Medway-type engines and was intended to both civil and military applications, but was not developed further than the drawings.

As so often in the VC10 story the genius of the design and many of its potential developments were wasted. The ultimate irony now lying in the recent procurement of remanufactured Boeing 707 airframes to meet military requirements for the RAF.

Seen from the cabin of an RAF VC10 K3, this RAF Jaguar got just about as close as you can get in-flight, as seen during the author's last RAF VC10 trip. Of note the VC10 wing panel displays the added saw-tooth vortex fence strakes which were a later Super VC10/K3 addition. Modellers should note such.

Other Operators

The original Super VC10 proposal with tip tanks, longer fuselage via front and rear 'plugs', as suggested to Pan Am in a variant form.

Vickers – soon to be within the BAC conglomerate – made sales pitches for the VC10 and Super VC10 all over the world in the desire to make a profit on the expensive-to-design and expensive-to-engineer VC10 project.

Smaller airlines were targeted alongside the major carriers. For example, Varanair of Siam (Thailand) was approached and liveries and a model Super VC10 created. Vickers sales teams made presentations to Egypt's Misrair, Aerolineas Argentinas, Lan Chile, with even a little-known approach to PLUNA of Uruguay in June 1961. In July 1961, Poland's airline, LOT, was also approached. A Super VC10 sales model in the colours of Greece's Olympic Airways was also created. As late as 1966, CSA of Czechoslovakia was approached (despite the politics inherent) and a demonstration flight in Prague took place, to no avail. As late as 1971, amid suggestions of selling DH/HS Tridents to China, a BAC sales team spoke to the Chinese about a possible VC10-licensed production series to be built in China, or restarting the Brooklands production line for an order of 120 airframes, but the British government failed to secure the project. With BAC 1-11 production sub-licensed to Romania, it was no surprise to see a VC10 sales pitch made to Bucharest.

Of note, the Royal Aircraft Establishment (RAE) MoD Experimental operated VC10 Fight Type 1102 XX914 which was ex-G-ATDJ of BCAL and was finally sent to RAF Brize Norton as test airframe 8777M.

The Pan Am VC10

A formal proposal to Pan American World Airways (Pan Am) was made in New York in 1960 of not just the Standard VC10 but also the proposed VC10 freighter variants. Vickers printed up a joint-logo Pan Am/Vickers brochure and technical review booklet. Clearly depicted therein was a planform view of a VC10 with wing leading-edge root fillets as an LR1 and as LR2 with trailing-edge fillets, both fillets housing extra fuel tanks. Wingtip fuel pods as seen on the Comet 4 were also cited. Removable cylindrical extra fuel tanks in the cargo hold could also add a safety margin for winter operations.

The 'Pan Am spec' VC10 could have carried 20,625 imperial gallons of fuel and might seat 196 Coach Class passengers for transcontinental US long-haul flights, or less in a two-class cabin for intercontinental flights. The BOAC Empire-route flight deck and its need for several extra officers could also be dispensed with – two crew operations being a new idea.

Vickers General Sales Manager (USA) Geoffrey Knight made a detailed technical presentation to Pan Am as early as 1960 and, provided lightly developed engines with better cruise fuel consumption could be secured (as suggested), the 'Pan Am Super VC10' with large main cabin, two crew and extra max-payload range, was quoted by Vickers to deliver a seat-per-mile cost of US$2.83 (average) and US$2.59 on a 4,000-mile non-stop sector. These highly competitive figures broke the

British United Airways in flight. Note some marking off the front cargo door and the revised wingtip design – not applied to the BOAC Standards. Safer stall margins at above FL40 were gained by the new wingtip shape.

US$3.45 cost on a short 500-mile sector. The airline took a serious look at this original Super VC10 proposal, but alas, it was not to be. Sadly, despite obvious economic improvements, the Super VC10 was not ordered by Pan Am. The key VC10 operators were to remain within British-influenced spheres.

Laker, BUA and Beyond

British United/British Caledonian Type 1103:

- ASIW *Loch Lomond*
- G-ASIX *Loch Maree*
- G-ATDJ *Loch Fyne*
- G-ARTA *Loch Ness*
  (Remanufactured Type 1100)

Sir Freddie Laker was a clever business-man, a pioneer and above all he was quick – he had to be to survive in a difficult market against larger players. So, while BOAC vacillated and pondered, Laker leapt on the VC10 bandwagon and made the most of the opportunity. In fact, the remanufactured VC10 Type 1100 prototype G-ARTA was subject of a Laker lease to become a BUA/BCAL airframe.

Laker's British United Airways had been talking to Vickers during the VC10 production stage and therefore can be given some credit as an important contributor to the VC10 story. Laker started the charter flight market which he and his BAC1-11 fleet would be part of creating. Laker flew cargo, people, in fact anything anywhere and that included troops on military charters. But in bidding for premier route licences, Laker and his on-paper Laker Airways and nascent British United entered a new world – one where they needed a smart and new jet. BUA had used second-hand Britannias and DC-6s. After being granted route licences to South America where Comets and 707s reigned, Laker did a deal with BAC (the Vickers name having by this time being subsumed into the new conglomerate) to purchase the VC10 modified to Laker's personal specifications with a cargo door.

With route licences awarded to South America and West Africa, Laker began to make good profits. He did so by offering a combination of flexibility of product and offered mixed cargo/freight and passenger opportunities by getting his VC10 equipped with the forward cabin cargo bay and a large upward-opening cargo door leading to a reinforced cabin floor. His VC10 could thus be a 'combi' configuration with 84 Economy Class seats and a large cargo bay. He could offer a small First Class cabin too. Alternatively, rearward-facing seats could be fitted throughout the whole cabin and Laker could service his MoD trooping contracts.

Laker's first production VC10 order for BUA was G-ASIX and it entered service on 31 July 1964 – not long after BOAC's 1101 model VC10s. Laker's machine had the revised wing leading-edge profile, 4 percent chord increase and new wingtip profiles. This specification was his VC10 Type 1103 and made the most of the improvements that BOAC had ignored, and which Ghana Airways had accepted on their first Type 1102 VC10. By October 1964, Laker's BUA had received G-ASIW which entered service just in time for Christmas of that year. Ghana Airways was very pleased with their first VC10 9G-ABO but did not take up the option of their second one which would have been registered 9G-ABQ. Laker seized the machine off the production line and it received an out-of-sequence registration as G-ATDJ.

BAC decided to try and recoup some of the money it had laid out for the VC10 programme and took the decision to fully renew its prototype VC10 airframe G-ARTA – that had appeared in BOAC's colours. After a refit that in-part was a rebuild and reconfiguration, a refreshed G-ARTA emerged – Freddie Laker smelled a bargain and pounced, but had to accept that it would not have the forward cargo door to his BUA specification. This aircraft was immediately leased to Middle East Airlines and wore their full livery as OD-AFA. It was later written off in British Caledonian colours during an empty landing at Gatwick in windy conditions in 1972. A previous

The British Caledonian livery with lion rampant, seen as far afield as South America and Africa.

One proposal was to create a short-haul VC10 for BEA (often cited in various versions as VC11). This Vickers drawing suggested a four-engined BEA VC10 with a longer fuselage and clipped wings – tailored to short-to-medium range high-cycle operations.

heavy landing had kinked the fuselage and stressed the rear end; it was deemed not economically viable to repair.

BUA's VC10s crossed the Andes (scene of a famous VC10 jet upset due to turbulence), dropped in to Nairobi, toured the shipping ports and cities of the Far East and on occasion even performed short-haul holiday charter flights in Europe. BUA VC10s also appeared in Sierra Leone titles after a 1960 agreement to set up that nation's new air service. Sierra Leone stickers were applied to Type 1103 G-ASIW as leased from BUA. Laker seized the opportunity to serve Sierra Leone Airways with a Britannia and then a BUA VC10 sporting the very large Sierra Leone titling as applied adhesive stickers. In late 1964 the VC10 G-ASIW embarked on a leased Sierra Leone-titled service that lasted into 1965, it is believed with that title painted onto the aircraft.

The Union Jack featured large in BUA's original livery, but was smaller in the airline's new BUA logo typed colour scheme of 1966. BUA served Argentina, Chile, Peru, Brazil and Uruguay – this was the oft-forgotten domain of BUA's all-white VC10s in remote corners of South America.

Laker and BUA worked the VC10s hard – with two airframes clocking up 3,000 flying hours in just 390 sectors. In 1970 BUA was absorbed by British Caledonian

and the BUA VC10 fleet soon reappeared in Caledonian's attractive blue livery with a large lion rampant upon the tailfin and with Scottish names applied. B-Cal, as it was tagged, used 707-320s on its long-haul routes, but continued to use the ex-BUA machines on South American and other services including to West Africa. After just under five years' hard work, the high-cycle and hard-worked VC10s were sold off.

Gulf Air and VIP VC10s

Gulf Air Type 1101:

- A40-VC
- A40-VG
- A40-VI
- A40-VK,
- A40-VL
- A40-AB Sultan of Oman Royal Flight Type 1103
- G-ARVJ Qatar Government Type 1101
- G-ARVF UAE Government Type 1101

Gulf Air began with DC-3s, yet expanded rapidly into jet aviation. By 1975 the convenient opportunity of BOAC becoming British Airways (BA) and the availability of its waning Standard-model VC10s which, although a decade old and hard-worked, were in excellent condition, well maintained and still had plenty of flight cycles left in

The stunning BAC-designed colour scheme of the East African fleet made the Super VC10 look even longer. Here is 5X-UVA in flight as captured by the BAC photographer. This aircraft crashed on take-off due to external factors, at Addis Abba in 1972.

them. Gulf Air had of course an Imperial Airways and BOAC history – BOAC owned shares in the company. Transferring its VC10s was not a huge challenge.

Having done a leasing deal in 1972 with BOAC for a VC10 to operate with 'Gulf Air' stickers applied to its noses for scheduled services to Bahrain from London Heathrow, in 1974, Gulf Air purchased five of the BOAC VC10 fleet and these came with a contingent of BOAC/BA VC10 pilots who were either transferred or directly employed on short-term contracts. The VC10s gave up their BOAC colours and emerged as all white with a triple-coloured stripe running from the nose and up the VC10's stylish tail. With a Gulf A-40 registration added in front of the former BOAC (British) registration, the original BOAC sub-registration lived on; as example, G-ARVC became A40-VC. Four A40 VC10s followed on.

After just three years of operations (which included a sublease of A40-VL to Air Ceylon to operate on Heathrow–Colombo services), Gulf Air went wide-bodied and ordered Lockheed Tristars. The VC10 fleet had just begun to appear in Gulf's new Golden Falcon livery; two of them sported the new paint scheme, but most of the fleet were wound down and were not painted – instead they were sold off to Dismore Aviation (brokers) in December 1977 and January 1978 prior to conversion to RAF K2 Type.

Gulf Air's A40-VL was, in early 1978, the last Standard VC10 in scheduled airline service. So popular was the VC10 in the Gulf States that no less than three airframes became the personal transport of local leaders. The government of Qatar purchased a lease on BOAC's G-ARVJ for the ruler's personal flight and the aircraft was eventually retired in 1981 and went to the RAF for conversion. BOAC's G-ARVF was sold to the United Arab Emirates government in 1974 and served with Sheikh Zayed as a stunning executive jet until 1981 prior to being preserved at the Hermeskeil Aviation Museum in Germany. The Sultan of Oman Royal Flight purchased G-ASIX from BCAL as A40-AB (he donated it back to Brooklands Museum at the end of its career on 6 July 1987). Equipped with lounges and double-bedrooms, this was a VC10 with a unique history.

East African Airways (EAA)

East African Airways Super VC10 Type 1154:

- 5X-UVA
- 5H-MMT
- 5Y-ADA
- 5X-UVJ
- 5H-MOG

The final, ultimate Type 1154 Super VC10s – including the last airframe built (5H-MOG) – were operated by East African Airways (EAA) rather than the originating order airline – BOAC itself. EAA ordered its new fleet in early 1965 and took rapid delivery with the first Super VC10, 5X-UVA arriving in 1966.

Boeing 707s had been looked at by EAA, but the company already had de Havilland Comet 4 experience and EAA's chairman was convinced of the Super VC10's abilities out of hot-and-high Nairobi and its (then) 5,320-foot-altitude runway. With the forward fuselage cabin cargo door added, along with all the aerodynamic refinements, and with B-spec Rolls-Royce Conway 43/550s that pumped out at least 22,500-lb thrust each, the EAA Super VC10s were the largest, most powerful and sleekest sight in African skies. They went like rockets.

EAA decided to make the most of everything about the Super VC10 being just that – super. Direct flights to and from Africa and Europe – fully loaded – were possible and the planned EAA service to New York just one refuelling stop away (planned for Zurich). EAA's Supers beat BOAC's Super VC10 into African skies – the latter's machines eventually tracking down to South Africa and the Seychelles/ Mauritius service, as well as crossing the Indian Ocean up to Singapore and then to Hong Kong.

For its variant of the Super VC10, EAA ordered a 14-seat First Class cabin and a 110-seat Economy Class: between the two lay the lucrative freight cabin that added to the export economy of East Africa, although this reduction (for more cargo capacity) did create an adverse seat-per-mile cost when such was seen in isolation.

Everything Vickers had learned went into the EAA Super VC10s and a new bold white livery was designed. The addition of multi-coloured side stripes made the Super VC10 look even longer than the dignified blue of BOAC, with the EAA blue lion emblem positioned just behind the cockpit windows.

The EAA Super VC10 fleet flew east to India and Asia – notably a Hong Kong service – and transited Zurich for London Heathrow. The Super VC10s also provided a high-quality service across Africa to Lagos and Accra. EAA used its Super VC10s to numerous European holiday destinations and in early operations tended to make the airliners stop more often than the task for which they had been designed – to the detriment of fuel and crew costings. This practice was soon modified. The concept and sight of a direct link between Nairobi and New York with a new Super VC10 was perhaps the greatest operational achievement of the EAA Super VC10 story: 5H-MOG flew the inaugural service on 10 December 1970 under the command of Captain G. Leslie. EAA also achieved the first sight of the Super VC10 in Australian and New Zealand skies in 1974, carrying the Kenyan team to the Commonwealth Games in New Zealand. The Super VC10 fleet was crewed by local, ex-pat and increasing numbers of indigenous African flight deck crews.

EAA's Super VC10 5X-UVA was EAA's first and flew from 12 October until it was written off in the take-off accident at Addis Abba on 18 April 1972 when a punctured nose wheel and subsequent events – airfield topography and placements – caused it to crash off the runway and burn out with many casualties but some survivors – the only Super VC10 accident.

The power, safety and style of the EAA Super VC10s carved a niche in African history. Sadly, EAA eventually went bankrupt on 27 January 1977 after several years of cashflow problems and unpaid bills and refused fuel carnets. The still-young fleet was promptly repossessed on account of overdue airframe payments and flown straight back to the UK where they then sat, dry-wrapped for a number of years prior to conversion with fuselage fuel tanks for the RAF air-to-air tanker fleet.

5H-MMT entered EAA service in October 1966 and, upon EAA's bankruptcy in 1977, was repossessed and ferried to Bristol Filton, latterly to be converted to RAF Type 1164 K Mk.3 as ZA147 – the last RAF VC10 airframe to fly. The EAA machines were flown back to Filton mostly under the captainship of Arthur Ricketts who then went on to update the VC10 rating of no less a figure than Brian Trubshaw. 5Y-ADA was sold to the RAF after repossesion. 5X-UVJ arrived in Nairobi in April 1969 and was repossessed in May 1977. It was sold to the RAF as a conversion. 5H-MOG was the last-ever built VC10 of any type – as an EAA Super VC10 – and was a child

of the 1970s, being completed in February 1970. It served just seven years with EAA before being repossessed to Filton in August 1977 and thence to the RAF as Type 1164 K.Mk.3 joining 101 Squadron in February 1985 as ZA150.

East African went for a bright and very 1970s interior colour palette and some wonderful wildlife murals on the cabin walls.

Ghana Airways

Ghana Airways Type 1102:

- 9G-ABO
- 9G-ABP

While ex-French colonies purchased Caravelles, the ex-British colony of Ghana purchased its first jet airliner – a Type 1102 Standard model VC10. This machine incorporated the improved wing leading edge and new wingtips that Vickers had readied early in the development process to improve lift and reduce drag.

Ghana Airways had been born in 1958 and was part-capitalized by BOAC and it was natural that after the Bristol Britannia which flew in Ghana Airways titles, that a VC10 order would be made. By 1961, under a new president, Ghana would see larger air traffic numbers between Accra and London and the airline ordered three VC10s in 1961. The latter two were to have the forward cargo door. By November the first 'GH' – Ghana Airways VC10 Type 1102 – had been delivered in a smart new livery designed at Brooklands. This aircraft, 9G-ABO, would shuttle between the two cities of Accra and London for 16 years without fuss or accident. An initial period of using British crews ended when Ghanaian pilots became fully qualified on the VC10. The VC10s ordered were underemployed and Ghanaian routes to America and the Middle East failed to materialize, so the two further GH VC10s were excess to the airline, with 9G-ABP being leased to MEA where it was damaged by munitions in Israeli military action at Beirut Airport in 1968 – a nearly new VC10 lost. The third GH machine went to BUA as G-ATDJ and an after-life with the British RAE/MoD. Yet the sole 9G-ABO was kept so busy that it had to be repainted by part process during scheduled maintenance – so it often appeared in non-standard colours even after a bright new livery was created in 1976.

A lovely view of the Ghana Airways 9G-ABO in the original livery, taken by the Vickers/BAC photographer in 1964 prior to delivery. Ghana was rightly proud of its incident-free VC10 operations.

Nigeria Airways

Nigeria Airways Type 1101:

- G-ARVI (leased from BOAC)
- G-ARVA leased then purchased as 5N-ABD

Ghana's neighbour, Nigeria, was also an ex-British colony, but one with a more troubled history. Again, it was natural that the emerging Nigeria Airways, so long a previous Imperial Airways/West African Airways arena, and a BOAC premier route, should be a VC10 application. Nigeria Airways ran to Lagos with BOAC providing the machinery and flight crew and Nigeria Airways supplying some cabin crews and ground services. The Nigeria Airways logo would be applied via adhesive stickers to the BOAC aircraft deployed to the route.

The Lagos run was a high-revenue route for BOAC and for Nigeria Airways (WT). Soon BOAC was jointly titled up for the BOAC/WT flights to West Africa. BOAC's G-ARVA and G-ARVI received the bright green and gold Nigeria Airways stickers on their noses as part of a wet-lease agreement. This led to a fully painted Nigeria Airways VC10 in green and white stripes. In 1969 Nigeria Airways purchased BOAC's G-ARVA – that airline's first VC10. It was registered as 5N-ABD and operated by a mix of ex-BOAC crews. Sadly, it crashed on final approach to Lagos on 20 November 1969 in circumstances of a let-down procedure and runway/air traffic control events that led to disaster with all on board perishing in the impact or, worse, in the ensuing fire. Of note, Nigeria Airways operated its VC10 in two colour schemes.

Air Malawi

Air Malawi Type 1103:

- 7Q-YKHG

By the early 1970s, the idea of Malawi having its own jet airliner service to Europe in order to serve its growing trade and international status, manifested in early 1974 in the lease of an ex-BUA, BCAL Standard VC10 service in which a BCAL-liveried VC10 operated an Air Malawi service from Gatwick to Blantyre and return, on a weekly basis. By the end of that year, BCAL had sold a Type 1103 ex-BUA VC10 (G-ASIW) to the Malawian government as 7Q-YKH. Painted up at Gatwick in an old-fashioned red and white livery, the machine became the flagship of the Malawian nation. The initial services began in December 1974 and saw good load figures. By late 1976, the idea of stopping en route at Amsterdam Schiphol was framed, the service beginning in early 1977.

A twice-weekly Air Malawi service to Gatwick and a local schedule to the Seychelles and other East African airports lead the sole VC10 accruing 60 hours a week in the air. This was asking a lot from a second-hand airframe, but 7Q-YKH did, in the main, perform well. Freight traffic soon gained a place in the economics of the service.

With rising fuel costs, engine and airframe overhauls, the Air Malawi VC10 chapter closed in September 1978. The aircraft went into storage at Bournemouth Hurn (where 7Q-YKH's tail had been built at the Vickers facility) for a long and expensive fallow period. With no buyer found, 7Q-YKH was flown back to Malawi after three years at Hurn. A major service, adding oils, changing tyres, running the electrics and hydraulics and days of ground runs allowed an Air Malawi crew to remove the VC10 on a Malawian airworthiness certificate back to Chileka via Athens. There, the VC10 sat for nearly a decade, deteriorating and becoming a hulk. It tipped over backward, falling onto her tail, and had to be righted. Then in 1995 7Q-YKH was chopped up for scrap. It was a sad end to the VC10 as part of African aviation.

Middle East Airlines

Middle East Airlines Type 1100/1102:

- OD-AFA (As leased ex-Laker)
- 9G-ABP (As lease ex Ghana Airways)

Middle East Airlines (MEA) had, under British spheres of influence, flown Comet

Air Malawi's sole VC10 (ex-BCAL) ran a regular service from 1974 to late 1978 without accident. Its red tail was a regular sight at Gatwick and Amsterdam.

The Sultan's machine comes home to Brooklands for final rest as a gift to the museum on 6 July 1987.

4s and Viscounts, so VC10 was natural territory for the Beirut-based airline. MEA had big ambitions – even transatlantic routes – but it failed to secure the licences it wanted. MEA was also unable to secure trade agreements with the British government that would have leveraged the funding for purchase of two or even three VC10s in 1966. So MEA became a Boeing 707 customer but it did lease two VC10s for a brief period.

Equipped in an unusual livery with a white body, thin red cheatline and the famous cedar tree logo on the fin, MEA's VC10 variation was very different indeed. Via use of the second Ghana Airways VC10 which was registered in Ghana as 9G-ABP and then leased to MEA two years later in 1967 but destroyed by military action at Beirut Airport on 28 December 1968, MEA had an unusual VC10 operation. The loss of 9G-ABP removed a nearly new, low-hours VC10.

The ex BUA/Laker VC10 remanufactured prototype G-ARTA was sub-leased to MEA and registered as such for use for 11 months in 1968 as OD-AFA, then going to BCAL again.

An unusual view of the ex-BUA/BCAL Type 1103 A40-AB of the Sultan of Oman, shows off the engine-mounting pods and tailfin designs. Now in need of a repaint.

VC10 Variants

Standard VC10 developments included:

- Type 1100 as baseline manufacturer's reference model nomenclature non-flying.
- Type 1101 BOAC'Standard VC10.
- Type 1102 & Type 1103 Standard Model VC10s.
- Standard model VC10s incorporating the revised wing with 4-percent chord increase and improved wing leading edge and new wingtips that Vickers had readied early in the development process to improve lift and reduce drag and to increase stall margin at over 40,00 feet.
- Type 1109 manufacturer's prototype G-ARTA reconfigured and refurbished to new standard in 1968.
- Type 1150 as baseline manufacturer's Super VC10 model nomenclature non-flying.
- Type 1151 BOAC Super VC10 .
- Type 1154 EAA Super VC10.
- Type 1106 RAF VC10 C.Mk.1 (latterly converted as Type 1180).
- Type 1112 RAF VC10 K.Mk.2.
- Type 1164 RAF VC10 K.Mk.3.
- Type 1170 RAF VC10 K.Mk.4.

Super and Not-so-Super: LR.1, LR. 2 and Super VC10

VC10 was ripe not just for engineering development and a bigger or rather a longer VC10 was planned via proposals in the Vickers Advanced Project Office. A high capacity version of the VC10 had been considered early on in 1959 – as a stretched Vanjet VC10 iteration. But could the stretch of the airframe be made to create an almost new version of the original? Could the VC10 contain enough reserves of performance and lifting ability to be reconfigured into a 200-plus-seater for use on the much easier transatlantic long-haul routes to New York, Los Angeles, San Francisco, Vancouver, or across the Pacific or on polar routes? Surely a bigger VC10 could sell to many airlines and make a valid base for a pure freighter? Either way, the bigger VC10 could have been, along with the DC-8 63, the longest, single-aisle non-wide-bodied airliner in the world.

Vickers developed the LR.1 and LR.2 VC10 variants as proposals – longer fuselages, more fuel tanks (including wingtip tanks) and some aerodynamics changes. Vickers also reckoned it could add underfloor fuel tanks and leading-edge or trailing-edge wing fillets housing 250 or 500 gallons of extra fuel and these ideas were initially the VC10 L.R.1 and L.R.2 types.

The operating range would be up to 5,000 miles and the cabin might seat 212 or even 220 passengers

Then came the big stretch – the Super VC10 200. This had a much longer forward fuselage (26 feet longer), a small stretch of the cabin behind the wings (hence 200 seats), more fuel tankage (including a tailfin tank), and, of note, larger cabin doors. Here then was a truc long-haul transatlantic big jet that could match, and indeed exceed, the larger 707 and the huge DC-60-series machines for operating economics.

Vickers were also working on a 265-seater VC10 Superb iteration – with a double-deck fuselage suggestion – a vastly expensive retooling of the entire forward and under fuselage design.

BOAC were offered the 200-seater Super VC10 200 – a machine solely designed for their easier routes to and from America such as London–New York, Boston, and London–Los Angeles non-stop. Los Angeles to Sydney with one stop was possible too. The proposed operating and seat-per-mile costs were highly competitive but the machine would not be viable on tropical routes – deliberately so. Super 200 was designed for making money on temperate region routes; it was not a hot-rod for Africa and Asia.

BOAC went for a compromise Super VC10 instead. They were interested in a more economic variant of the VC10 – something less powerful with more seats to sell – but then, contrary to what it said it needed across the Atlantic, BOAC suggested a more modest Super VC10 – a shorter stretch. So took root the idea of watering the Super 200 concept down so that the new, higher-seat-capacity Super VC10 could still *also* be used on more difficult BOAC routes. It seemed to be another BOAC paradox – wanting a more economic, higher-capacity Super VC10, but then demanding that such formula was watered down so that the new airliner could still retain capabilities on routes that it was specifically designed for – or redesigned *not* to perform on. Vickers was frustrated again: here was the bigger VC10 to tackle the transatlantic routes that BOAC had wanted, but BOAC wanted a smaller, bigger VC10!

There seemed little point of a dual-ability Super VC10 that was neither one thing nor the other. Such a machine might not tackle the seat-per-mile-cost operating economies of the larger 707 and DC-8 as well as could otherwise be managed. But this is exactly the Super VC10 that BAOC demanded – a weaker, smaller, larger VC10 with worse operating and seat-profit costs than the massive Super 200 that was possible and was offered by Vickers.

Key Super VC10 engineering/design changes:

- 156-inch fuselage extension.
- 75 inches between forward fuselage and 81 inches at rear fuselage.
- Structural keel member stiffened to take longer forward fuselage loads to avoid nose-nodding.
- Top skin fuselage panels thickened in strategic locations.
- Curvature changes to nose-fuselage joins.
- Increases to metal gauges in wings and wheel-well locations.

Seen here in model form, the proposed true BAC Super VC10 200 was a major redesign using longer fuselage, larger doors, strengthened wing, stronger undercarriage beams and uprated engines. It traded performance for payload-range and could have competed against the DC8-60-series 200-seater very effectively. But launch costs were high and BOAC thought it too 'super' so opted for a constrained Super VC10 specification.

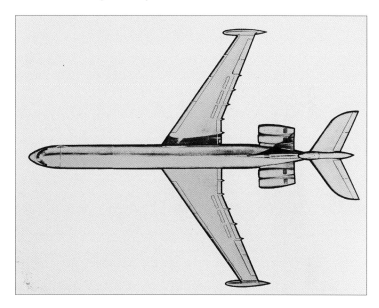

VC10 LR.1 and LR.2 were long-range variants with longer fuselages and wingtip tanks of 250 gallons each. A swing-nose, front-loading freighter version was also planned. The ideas did not get further than the drawing board.

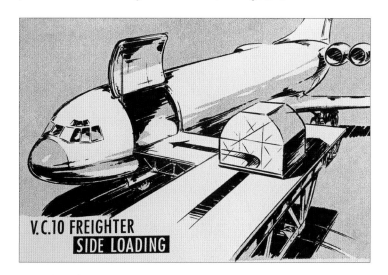

A complete all-cargo and part-cargo combi version of the VC10 family was designed and costed by Vickers but the funds to launch it build it did not materialize despite some very real interest shown in this, the world's first true, dedicated cargo-system airliner design.

The very rare, raised upper deck VC10-type freighter had clamshell loading doors, a cockpit bubble and massive potential. It too was not built. This is the only known rendering of it – as an original Vickers model.

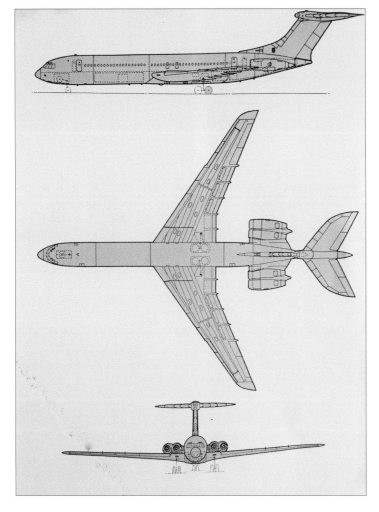

The BOAC Super VC10 seen in three-view drawing as type 1151 and as EAA Type 1153. The very large main wing and tailplane are clearly evident.

- Rear cargo door relocated.
- Minor cockpit and crew station layout changes.
- Forward galley and toilet location changes.
- Engine nacelle angle changed by 3 degrees and four thrust reversers (two later removed due to buffet to tailplane).
- Uprated Conway B engines on wider stub wing to 11 in and reshaped pods
- Interior trim changes.
- New 14.5-degree flap setting for take-off.

At 171 feett 8 inches (52.32 m) long and with a maximum take-off weight of 335,000 lb (151,958 kg), Super VC10 was the biggest and heaviest airliner ever made in Europe at that time. It was also the most powerful until the later-model Boeing 747 with RB211 524 engines. VC10 and Super VC10 were the fastest airliners of their era with a high-speed Super VC10 cruise speed of 505 kts (582 mph/936 km/h) at 31,000 feet (9449 m). Higher altitudes (> 36,000 feet) saw both VC10 and Super VC10 exceed the 600 mph/966 km/h figure. Super VC10 was up to 15 kts faster in the cruise than the 707-320B thanks to the aerodynamic advantage – but Super VC10's added weight meant a bit more fuel burn once settled into long-range cruise.

BOAC ordered the Super VC10 design as their definitive Super VC10 and used it to create a marketing offering for the transatlantic, round-the-world and Pacific routes, but the chance of 200 seats and even lower costs had been lost (the DC-8 60 series would fill that gap). The first Super VC10 test flight was on 7 May 1965, just one month after the Standard VC10 had entered service.

The Super VC10 could manage over 9 hours in flight with a 9 hours 50 minutes endurance in typical flight conditions – depending on winds and allotted heights (but with possibly lower fuel reserves). According to BOAC's own official Statement of Accounts in 1971, the Super VC10 fleet had worked 12 hours a day, every day (in the air) by flying 70,347 hours at an average of 4,387 hours per airframe.

The BOAC Super VC10s (Type 1151) were registered G-ASGA – G-ASGR.

From 29 April 1964 to October 1976, the BOAC/BA Standard VC10 June flew revenue-earning 409,405 hours and the Super VC10 fleet, from 1965 to March 1981, flew 797,791 flying hours without accident or injury. VC10 G-ARVM was the last of the fleet to be built and the last to remain in BA service beyond 1976. The Super VC10's last scheduled commercial airline flight was from the Indian Ocean islands to Dar es Salaam and Larnaca to London Heathrow on 29 March 1981 with G-ASG ending the BOAC/BA VC10 and Super VC10 story. There followed two chartered enthusiasts' flights around the UK airports and BAC factory sites over the next few days.

- Strengthened landing gear side-stay frame and reinforced landing gear.
- Fin fuel tank structural skin wet fin with 1,350-gallon (6,173-l) capacity with force-feed ram air.
- Change to outboard wing fence and additional mini-fences and vortex sections.
- Maximum speed for 45-degree flap increase to 184 kts.
- Addition of rear fuselage cabin door; removal of mid-cabin door.
- Forward cabin doors and service doors repositioned.

VC10 Superb 265 and cargo capacity VC10s

There were many proposals for the development of the VC10 airframe. Two of the most important that never saw flight were the Superb and the Freighter designs.

This proposal saw the VC10 fuselage deepened and an 80-seat lower deck cabin forward of the wing leading into a reprofiled nose. 265 seats were proposed; a variant with closer-seat pitch might offer 80 seats downstairs and 200 on the main deck. All doors, windows, wings and tail parts and main structural items would be carried over and the double-bubble lower deck would effectively be a multi-arc mirror of the existing fuselage design. Rolls-Royce RB178 high-bypass fan engines (x 2) were suggested – as precursors to the famous RB211.

In May 1965, yet another British aviation minister had the unenviable task of telling the House of Commons that VC10 funding – in this case up to £50 million for the launch of the VC10 Superb 265 – was not to be forthcoming.

VC10 F3–F4, the freighters that never were

Perhaps the most intriguing 'loss' of what might have been for the VC10, concerned the VC10 freighter or cargo versions. Most observers know that a forward-hinged fuselage design for the VC10 was created, but few were aware that the clamshell-type, upper-lobed, nose-loading freight design was considered and a model made.

With its performance reserves, the VC10 airframe offered very good freight/cargo payloads. Removing the cabin seats, trims, galleys and toilets of the passenger-specification VC10 reduced weight and added payload ability.

A VC10 F3 (F for Freighter) side-loading design proposal had made the most of the RAF-type reinforced floor and side cargo door. F3 might carry an incredible 80,000-lb payload.

The further F4 freighter variant added a nose-loading facility by having a swing-nose section. F4 used a hydraulically hinged and clamped forward section and plug-type controls and service mechanisms to ensure the flight deck was secured when closed and control runs protected.

Vickers envisaged special loading ramps and jacking platforms to be part of a global freight network package, allowing quick loading and unloading of the F4. A 15-minute turnaround was quoted if using the dedicated ground equipment. This freighter could lift 79,000 lb over 3,500 miles. The maximum freight package size was 82 feet – at that time the world's largest proposed air-cargo volume. A heavy-duty >1,000 lb/ft^2 floor strength could also be specified – at weight penalty.

Lesser known was the VC10 clamshell-type nose loading freighter that featured

VICKERS **VANJET**

a Carvair-type, or Boeing 747-style upper deck 'bubble' and elevated flight deck station – below which a cavernous >95-foot cargo deck was offered. Although it got off the drawing board to model stage, the double-decked, clamshell-nose required an expensive new fuselage structure and, although decades ahead of its time, was not pursued. Only Boeing's 747F would rival it over a decade later.

Mixed passenger and cargo combi schemes were also suggested for VC10. These and the pure-freighter VC10s were well ahead of today's massive market for such cargo airframes.

Such VC10 schemes, like the Super 200, the Superb and the freighters, were the lost future of the VC10.

Top: The famous T-tail seen in the Super VC10 with its longer engine stub-wing mountings taking the pods further away from the fuselage to reduce interference drag and boundary-layer effects.

Above: The Vickers jet freighter cargo liner started on the drawing board in the 1950s with the idea for a Vanjet cargo airframe with forward cargo door. Vanjet out of Vanguard, became VC10.

Standard VC10 of British Overseas Airways Corporations (BOAC) seen in the airline's original 1950s style livery as seen on everything from a Comet to a Constellation. The original design was believed to have stemmed from proposals by the British industrial designer Robin Day. The white Speedbird emblem continued the 1930s design that had been applied to Imperial Airways machines of that era. From the VC10 Type 1100 prototype G-ARTA and onto the BOAC Type 1101 series, this early livery appeared, but was soon superseded from early 1964 onwards. An expensive, early repaint of some of the pre-delivery machines was required.

In April 1964 the Standard VC10 operated its first revenue-earning service (to Lagos, Nigeria). G-ARVY featured this new livery for that service. The livery shown here depicts the golden Speedbird on the tailfin, but displaying the new cheatline design that was stepped in a curious manner on the forward fuselage. The cheatline was edged in bright gold stripes and the BOAC title moved to the lower forward fuselage. This livery was, arguably, the least popular of the BOAC VC10 schemes and was short-lived being in service for less than 12 months. Of note to modellers, this livery, briefly seen on the first BOAC Super VC10 G-ASGC in March 1965, was modified before revenue-earning service entry.

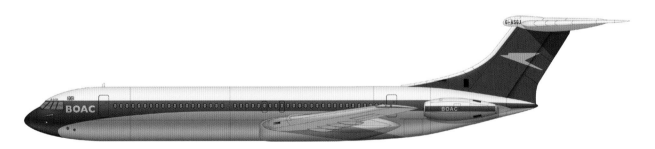

The defining BOAC Speedbird livery with elegant curved forward cheatline shape and large bolder fonts and emblems seen applied to the Super VC10. The initial version had dark blue strakes applied from the base of the tailfin on each side which ran forward onto the upper fuselage but these were soon deleted as their visual effect was minimal. It was the old-fashioned nature of the stepped-cheatline livery that led to this final and defining revision for the 1960s. Because the Super VC10 was longer, the lengthening effect of the livery was even more noticeable. This livery became the icon of BOAC and was applied across its fleet right up to its early Boeing 747 airframes of the pre-1974 BOAC era. It is generally agreed to look its best on the stunning lines of the VC10 and particularly the Super VC10. BOAC advertising made the most of this inspired livery design. Note the differing livery applied to the engines as compared to the earlier BOAC schemes.

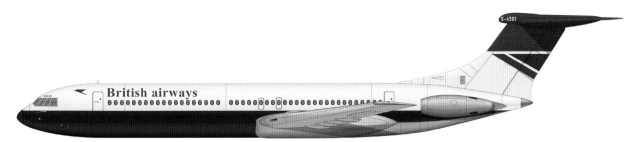

Designed by the Negus agency, this fly-the-flag British Airways livery was applied to the Super VC10 fleet and notably to the Standard VC10 G-ARVM as the Super VC10 service back-up airframe based at London Heathrow. The previous branding mark of dominance, the Speedbird, is reduced to a small emblem on the upper forward fuselage – with a large-scale depiction of the Union Jack applied to the fin. To save weight and time, the dark blue undersides did not apply fully to the lower section of the fuselage from the nose wheel back. The engines lacked any company or Rolls-Royce emblems. A Royal Mail emblem was applied (aft of the forward fuselage door) to the first repaint in this livery. The white fin base would reveal exhaust effluence soot marks in service.

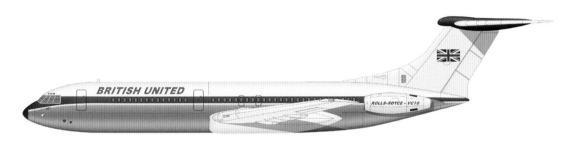

Rolls-Royce VC10. Freddie Laker was proud to offer the Standard VcC10 in competition to the state-supported national carrier that was BOAC. Sir Freddie as he became, would even transport his Rolls-Royce Silver Cloud car in the forward freight hold on sales tours for his airline. This livery shows the early British United livery that first flew on G-ASIW on 30 July 1964. A very dark blue (almost black) cheatline is edged in beige and the national flag is small on the tailfin. The early British United VC10s (with main deck forward cabin cargo doors) ranged far and wide on schedules, charter and trooping service and made visits to African and Asian airports that had not then seen a BOAC VC10 or any VC10. The early livery saw the short-lived Sierra Leone titling as agreed on an early code-share type arrangement with that country by Laker.

Bright, bold BUA and not unlike Freddie Laker himself. This was the new post-1966 livery design applied by Laker to his entire fleet of aircraft. This was a more 1970s' era graphic and font with BUA seen large on the double cheatline and on the tailfin as the cheatline ran upwards from the window line into the fin. Of note, the lower fuselage was of light grey paint finish. Sadly the Rolls-Royce VC10 logo was soon left off the engine pods as maintenance affected its lettering and line-up. By the close of 1970, BUA's merger with BCAL would spell the end of Laker's defining BUA livery and the moving on of Laker himself.

Seen circa 1972 with the tailfin lion rampant in a clever and modern scheme for its era and yet one still reflecting the airline's Scottish roots and senior management. This depiction shows the Standard VC10 in the hybrid markings after Caledonian and British United Airways (BUA) had merged in late 1970. The double-width cheatline was unusual at the time. BCAL Standard VC10 fleet were named after Scottish lochs: G-ASIW – *Loch Lomond*, G-ASIX – *Loch Maree*, G-ATDJ – *Loch Fyne*, G-ARTA – *Loch Ness*. VC10s of BCAL ranged far and wide from West Africa to South America including a three-times a week service across the South Atlantic to Argentina and then after refuelling over the Andes to Chile, in an often ignored chapter of VC10 operations. Brazil had refused BCAL permission to land or transit Brazil's own homebase and airline hub.

Totally different from the more formal BOAC Super VC10, the East African Airways (EAA) livery reflected in its three colours the elements of Africa – people, sun, soil and natural flora and fauna. The cheatline widened towards the rear emphasising the Super VC10's tail and made the Super look even longer. Fully painted underneath, the paint added weight but improved airflow. The flags and registration of EAA's respective owning partner were featured on the aircraft. Of note the tailplane and bullet fairing were painted light grey not white. Five Super VC10's were delivered to EAA – into the year of 1970. One airframe was lost in a take-off accident that was not the fault of the crew nor of the aircraft. EAA Super VC10s got to Sydney and to New York via Zurich as the first indigenous long-haul premier airliner service to America from Africa. Everyone in East Africa was proud of EAA, but the story ended badly. The aircraft went on to conversion as RAF tankers.

1964 saw the first of three Standard Type 1102 VC10s for Ghana Airways but only two were delivered. 9G-ABO was delivered in late November 1964 in the first livery, which was created for the airline by an external partner. Ghana Airways operating mainly on Accra–London via Rome or another stop, used three livery styles on its VC10s, not two as is often stated. The first 1964 livery featured a dark-coloured lower rudder panel, and white and red mid and upper rudder panels as part of a national flag depiction. Small Ghana Airways titles were applied to the mid-fuselage. By 1968, new, bolder titles had been applied to the forward fuselage and a brighter flag colour applied to each rudder section on the tailfin. Yet the thin blue cheatline remained in this the second livery.

After 1967, with low passenger traffic figures, Ghana only had one VC10 in service as 9G-ABP had been leased to Middle East Airlines (then destroyed by armed Israeli attack). It repainted the 9G-ABO in the bolder 1975–1980 in-service livery as a third livery that was launched in 1975. This saw a much brighter treatment, a large national flag rendered on the tailfin and an early use of an (almost) all-white fuselage treatment without cheatline and with brightly coloured main cabin doors. Modellers are offered many livery options via the staged application of the final Ghana Airways livery.

Seen as the first of two Nigerian liveries applied to an ex-BOAC Standard VC10, Nigeria Airways initially used a BOAC blue and gold VC10 with 'In service for Nigeria Airways' or Nigeria Airways stickers applied to the aircraft and covering the forward BOAC logo on the cheatline. Nigeria Airways, having received British government encouragement, had ordered two VC10s in 1961 but cancelled the order due to low passenger traffic numbers. Yet a Nigeria Airways logo was stuck onto a leased BOAC VC10 and operated to Lagos not long after BOAC's own services to Lagos had begun. BOAC supplied a wet-lease of airframe, crew and maintenance. G-ARVA and G-ARVI were the mainstay of this lease operation. In 1967 Nigeria Airways leased G-ARVC from BOAC but applied its own green and white colours with an unusual tailfin emblem of a Nigerian national flag abstract. This was the first Nigeria Airways livery. A small, flying elephant logo was of interest to many – seen on the forward fuselage. Nigeria then purchased, not G-ARVC (returned to BOAC after 12 months service in Nigerian colours) from BOAC, but G-ARVA. The second, starker, green-and-white Nigeria Airways livery with a double-striped narrow-width cheatline design, was then applied to 5N-ABD as this airframe had been re-registered for 1969. It was lost in the first-ever VC10 accident, on final approach to Lagos in late November 1969 amid a complex set of operating circumstances.

A popular and unique VC10 operation and livery, the Air Malawi Standard VC10 7Q-YKH was the last VC10 to grace African skies in 1978 and sadly was abandoned to its fate at Malawi's main airport from 1979 to the 1990s, eventually being stripped for scrap metal. Formerly BUA/BCAL airframe G-ASIW, with the cargo door option and wing updates, it was in late 1974 painted up in the stunning bright red of Air Malawi and began 'air malawi' operations all over Africa and Europe – being a regular sight at Amsterdam Schiphol, Nairobi and London Gatwick. The very bold titles and red fin created a high-visibility look that was set off by a widening cheatline front to rear. Modellers have turned to this unusual livery and 26 Decals produced a limited-edition decal set.

Depicted here is the original 1974-era Gulf Air livery showing the leased airframe's BOAC registration on the fin top prior to final A40 series registration after full fleet purchase. This very bold, tri-stripe livery launched Gulf Air's international VC10 services and was noteworthy for its golden titling in bold font on the upper fuselage. Five ex-BOAC Standards were used by Gulf Air – with BOAC flight crews then direct employment crews. Gulf Air created its Golden Falcon livery and service and VC10 operations from Bahrain to London commenced on 1st April 1974 using what it called the world's most passenger-preferred long-range airliner.

Only two of the five ex-BOAC VC10s in the Gulf Air fleet received the second and characterful Golden Falcon livery that actually featured a golden falcon emblem. These two airframes were A40-VL and A40-VL. The emblem was applied from 1977. With a triple-striped forward livery treatment and a massive golden falcon with unfalcon-like wings, depicted upon the fin, this was a stunning late 1970s livery that was seen on the last scheduled airline, Standard VC10 services into Heathrow in 1978. Of note, Air Ceylon titles were added to A40-VI as it was sub-leased to Ceylon/Sri Lanka for services from Columbo, including to London Heathrow.

Middle East Airlines, who had initially wanted to order three Super VC10s to establish its international network, then operated two VC10s. 9G-ABP which was the second-ordered Ghana Airways Type 1102 that was lightly used from 1965, was leased out to MEA in April 1967. Wearing the full MEA Cedar Tree livery and Air Liban subtitles, it was a rare beast. The thin red cheatline and white tail design were of the era. Sadly the airframe was damaged by weapons in an Israeli attack upon MEA's homebase Beirut Airport on 28 December 1968 whilst still almost new. The VC10 prototype G-ARTA was leased from Laker Airways to MEA in January 1968 as OD-AFA for 12 months; OD-AFA would return safely to London Gatwick for BCAL use, until damaged in a landing event. Depicted here is the baseline application of the MEA livery with the airline's titles in English on the outer engine pod, as opposed to Arabic script as seen on 9G-ABP.

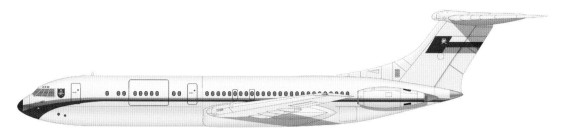

1975 saw an ex-BUA/BCAL Standard VC10 Type 1003 G-ASIX, sold to the Oman government in October 1974 for use by the Sultan of Oman. Registered as A40-AB, this airframe received a VIP interior with state room, bunks, falcon equipment for royal falconers and a very unusual livery with a grandly swept nose-to-tail cheatline below the window line. A shield emblem was hand painted on the forward fuselage. Maintained in the UK, flown by ex-RAF crews, this airframe became a regular visitor to London and other destinations and remained in service as a VIP transport until as late as July 1987 when it was donated by the Sultan to the Brooklands Museum Trust – where it had been constructed. Of interest to modellers, was that for some months into 1975 (in its early Omani life), A40-AB was operated still in its basic BCAL colours but with the titles and lion removed. The repaint appeared in October 1975.

Ex-BOAC Standard VC10 G-ARVF was sold to the United Arab Emirates in July 1974 and today rests in a West German museum. Of note, BOAC's G-ARVJ had been leased to the Qatari government as a VIP/Royal Flight aircraft from late 1975 to 1981. G-ARVF was used by the UAE right up to 1981. Its detailed livery and tailfin artwork were extremely popular as was the airframe itself. The very large bird of prey (with Arab Dhow inset) on the fin and Arabic script on the fuselage were all part of a livery designed at BA and then applied by the artisans in BA's paint shop. Expert modellers will revel in the details of this intricate and unusual livery.

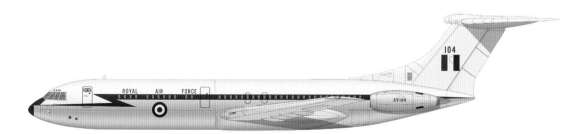

The classic Royal Air Force livery in white with a blue cheatline with Z-section design at the nose. All RAF VC10s bore the name of a Victoria Cross holder and several airframes saw dual VC holder titles and changes between airframes. Alternatively entitled, Transport Command, Support Command, but always with Royal Air Force titles on the forward fuselage, this famous livery was seen from 1966 through to 10 Squadron's last white VC10 operations in the 1990s. Many VC10 enthusiasts feel that beside the BOAC gold and blue, this RAF livery shows off the VC10's lines at their best. Various changes to the livery took place, notably the addition of Red Cross markings. An addition of the in-flight refuelling probe was a later commonality. The white livery lasted into the RAF VC10 C1K operations. Of note to modellers, the ex-RAF-liveried airframe ZR809, then to be registered G-AXLR and fitted with one RB211 high bypass jet engine to the port side, makes a good modelling subject and wore the titles ROLLS-ROYCE RB211 FLYING TEST BED, but was in basic RAF colours.

Shown with the very rare camouflage livery, the K2, ZA141 was the first of the tanker conversions to fly in such colours and rarely seen in such scheme beyond its early flights of June 1982. The disruptive camouflage of grey/blue and green was the subject of an Airfix kit, but is not widely popular with modellers, although it is very unusual. Seen in MoD and RAF publicity material of the time, this livery featured a rather unwise white underside to the wings and fuselage – not ideal in a military airframe and likely to become stained and degraded very quickly.

The famous RAF hemp livery and as applied to the airframes in early use by the ex-EAA Super VC10 tanker version at 101 Squadron from 1993, and also to the shorter VC10 types then deployed. Early VC10 K2 life cycles saw use of the hemp scheme across several theatres of operations including in the Gulf wars. The centre-line HDU refuelling points were often enhanced with high-visibility markings of black and white designs and mouths to offer guidance to refuelling fighters. Tailfin codes and non-standard markings added at operational level often appeared on these airframes.

The ex-EAA and certain ex-BA Supers, were, as RAF machines in K3 and K4 guises, sprayed in the excellent grey hue of their final service years. This was not glossy, but seemed semi-matt. Of note a pale blue, Z-cheatline flash was added to certain airframes in 1994–1995 which proved controversial in some military eyes. It is depicted here. In the main, the fleet were, up to October 2013, seen in the grey livery but with (or without) a dark grey Z-cheatline – or no cheatline at all. Ex-BA Super VC10s such as KMk.4 ZD235 and ex-EAA ZA 148, 149, and 150 were ultimately seen in all-grey colours. Modellers should note that this all-grey RAF late VC10 service finish featured a small band of the lower, under fuselage, underwing and outer HDUs, painted matt light grey. However some of the earlier KMk.2 series were indeed totally grey. Modellers need to source reference material and operational datelines to secure accurate renditions of such livery options.

As late as June 2012, four C1Ks were still active, four K3s were active and a single remaining K4 (ZD241) was in use – having been based at Port Stanley Mount Pleasant with the 1312 Refuelling Flight. 20 September 2013 saw the last-ever operational RAF VC10 flights after a 47-year career. Having replaced the unpopular light blue stripe design (of 1994) with a more fitting dark grey stripe, the K3s and K4s flew to the end in this livery (as depicted here). Note the deletion of alternate and other cabin windows.

XV105, withdrawn from service in late 2011 and scrapped in 2012, was formerly named *Arthur Scarf VC* and *Albert Ball VC*. It was transferred from 10 Squadron to 101 Squadron and is depicted as the converted RAF C Mk.1K – or K1 for short, as painted up in 2005 with a stunning black tailfin with golden markings, and engine script, to celebrate 101 Squadron's 90th Anniversary in fine style. With the K2 tankers the first to be retired, several of the K1s lingered until 2012. XV105 is the airframe and livery also celebrated in the Sky Classics model range (see modelling section). Of interest, XV104 was seen in 2012 with RAF Benevolent Fund crests and nose markings.

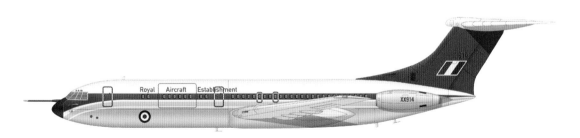

Given that some of the original VC10 aerodynamics development work took place at the Royal Aircraft Establishment (RAE) wind tunnel at Bedford, there was perhaps something ironic in the fact that VC10 should end up being transferred to the RAE Aero Flight. In 1973, the former Ghana Airways-ordered Standard VC10 Type 1002 9G-ABQ that was not delivered, and then registered as G-ATDJ, was passed to the RAE for flight trials and blind-landing category equipment development work registered as XX914. It had spent its airline life from 1965 with BUA and then BCAL as *Loch Fyne* and led a very interesting existence. The special RAE livery was of high-visibility type and unique but followed the BCAL paint lines. It was scrapped in 1983 but its forward fuselage went to Brize Norton as a training frame.

Modelling the VC10

The RAF's all-white VC10 C.Mk.1 of Transport Command is a modeller's favourite. Here the Corgi 1/144 model in metal is captured at a suitable flight angle.

VC10 in Model Form

The VC10 has been the modeller's favourite for decades. The first true VC10 model was Vickers' own wooden model VC10, one of which was carved and painted up in BOAC colours for the VC10 contract-signing ceremony. The first mass-produced VC10 model was a small 4-inch-long VC10 shape moulded in plastic and coloured BOAC gold and given away to First Class passengers on board BOAC VC10s.

One the nicest and rarest VC10 models was the 1973-issued BOAC VC10 at 1/250 in metal with retractable undercarriage made in Japan by Masudaya as Metal Scale Models Aero Mini range. Today this is one of the rarest VC10 collectables and commands very high prices.

A large number of kits and die-cast models have appeared over the years with varying degrees of accuracy. From plastic to alloy and in wood, VC10s and Super VC10s have appeared in scales ranging from 1/172, 1/144 to larger models. A man named Terry Mason has been flying a large-scale radio-controlled model VC10 for some years to great effect.

For the modeller, the VC10 website AlittleVC10derness at www.VC10.net, superbly created by Dutch pilot and engineer and Brooklands Museum trust supporter, Jelle Hieminga, is a vital research and reference tool for all VC10 details at scale and for the real thing.

In 2020, a new 1/72-scale VC10 model was launched by French model manufacturer Mach 2 Models. Available in the BOAC livery and in two RAF VC10 K2 liveries (camouflage and low-visibility grey). Although well detailed and made, the nose and cockpit window contours do seem slightly inaccurate. Despite this caveat, it is a superb model but one slightly affected by apparently inaccurate nose contours which may be able to be modified by the keen enthusiast.

The first accessible model kits were the resin/plastic offerings from Airfix and Frog which were on the market as the 1970s dawned. At one stage a Frog version with illuminated lights was available. Over 20 kit and built-model individual releases have been manufactured and are listed herein.

The Corgi Aviation Archive released a series of metal-cast VC10 models in RAF and BOAC liveries. Although not self-build kits, the excellent detailing and accuracy, and sales success and subsequent values, makes it appropriate to frame the Corgi model as our showcase VC10 example.

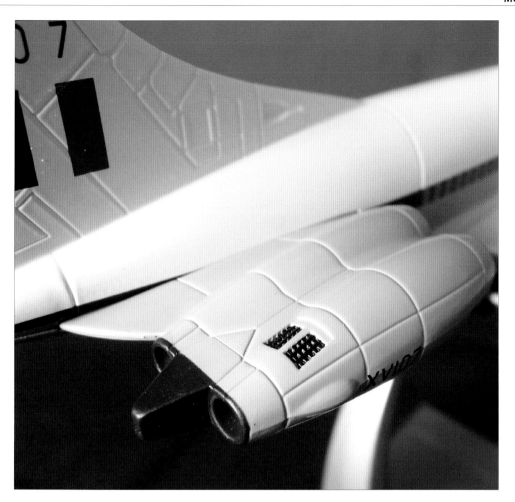

The initial casting and tooling had a small issue with the cabin windows. Here, the engine and tailfin details are displayed.

CORGI 1/144

First Release: AA37001/ Vickers VC10 C.Mk.1 of No. 10 Squadron RAF Brize Norton as Falkland Islands Casevac Service 1982 livery as 25th Anniversary release.

Expertly detailed in the main metal casting, the initial release of an RAF No. 10 Squadron in RAF white colours (with Casevac decals and Red Cross) seemed a great boost for VC10 enthusiasts. However, the first tooling used a separate cockpit roof section casting which gave an unfortunate and inaccurate appearance to the model. Corgi soon addressed this for subsequent releases – which featured the RAF hemp scheme and a subsequent BOAC blue and gold liveried edition.

Corgi, unlike some manufacturers, got nearly all the details correct – notably the shape of the fin, its bullet fairing and the tailplane. Despite the initial nose/fuselage casting issue, the contours were correct. The only real demerit was the shape of the windows. Somehow Corgi got the oval shape too square. Other details from leading edge to engine nacelles were all correct however. Crucially, the vital inboard wing fence *was* featured.

The Corgi range developed through Corgi's own changes. All three models were of limited edition numbers:

- XV107, VC10 C.Mk.1, RAF Brize Norton, Falklands 25th

Anniversary, production run limited to 1,810 models.
- ZA140, VC10 K.Mk.2, RAF Brize Norton, Military Air Power, production run limited to 1,054 models.
- G-ARVM, Standard VC10, British Airways, BA Heritage Collection, production run limited to 754 models.

Some issues with decals, cargo door locations and the rendition of the fuel hose pods and underbelly were noted on the RAF K.Mk.2. model.

Available on its wheels or gear-up or gear down on a stand, the model was improved upon in its subsequent BOAC livery release and this Corgi model range is now of increasing value in the marketplace.

The cargo door frame and cabin window shape were weaker elements of the original Corgi rendition. But overall, it did capture the essential elements of VC10 design.

Despite some minor detail detractions, the Corgi 1/144 die-cast metal model captured the essential design elements of the VC10 well. Here, the correct wing stance and dihedral are shown.

Above: Tailfin focus. The panel work, rudders and engine stub wing are well rendered.

Right: The vital, fin-top bullet or swan fairing is a key factor for any model of the VC10 and accurate curvatures and sections are essential if the VC10's true elegance is to be accurately captured. Many models fail to capture the VC10 tail details adequately.

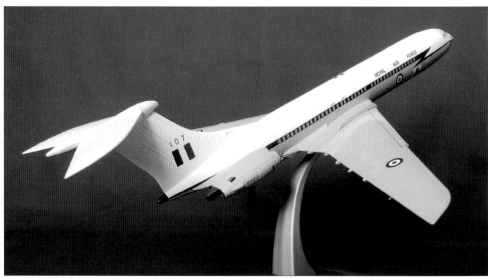

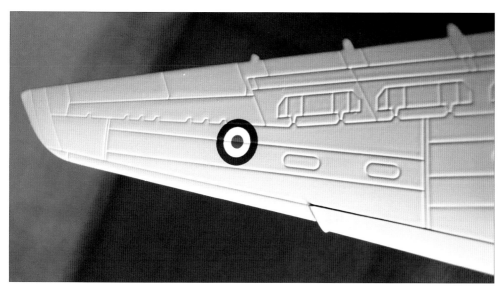

Main wing details. The leading-edge slats, flaps and airbrakes are all well-defined. The essential inboard fence is presented – often it is omitted from VC10 kits due to moulding or casting difficulties. Not so here. The correct developed-wing aerofoil and leading edge of the Super VC10 wing as applied to the RAF machines are accurate.

Seen from underneath, the model offers further accuracy on the underside. Wheel wells and gear doors are nicely scaled.

The engine pods are superb – yet are rendered in moulded plastic not metal – not that you can tell.

Gear down and in climb pose set on its plastic stand, the Corgi model Issue 1 was soon to be improved upon.

Above: The Corgi VC10 seen in 2nd Issue with the very rare earlier BOAC livery. Apart from some poor fuselage castings, the model was well received and is a collectors' item. Panel work is well captured by Corgi in this model but the cabin window shape is incorrect.

Right: The Corgi airframe detailing is depicted in this shot of the tailplane. Note the engine exhaust details and later, single thrust reverser per pod configuration – inboards having been deleted.

Model Market and Products

From classic plastic kits and injection-moulded, across vac-formed, wood and die cast, VC10 is well catered for. For the model maker, Airfix, Roden and Welsh Models currently populate the recent new/used kit market, as does a range of VC10 decal suppliers, and wooden model suppliers. Herpa metal 1/500 VC10s are rightly popular.

The Gemini Jets 1/400 collection has created a wonderful record of VC10 types, liveries and schemes – notably across the RAF VC10 incarnations. Other smaller-scale metal models include Jet-X Super VC10 1/400; a recent edition in the 1/200-scale market is JC Wings. Aero Classics issued a 1/400 Super VC10 in metal, as did Inflight 500 at 1/500 scale.

VC10 enthusiasts with deep pockets can of course purchase earlier large-scale wooden display models or more recent wooden display models (some are excellent, others fail to accurately render the correct shapes and forms of the VC10). The ultimate must of course be to source a 1960s Westaway travel agency/airline display glass fibre model of the VC10 with scales of 1/72, 1/24 and a handful of 1/16 at over 10 feet long with a glazed cutaway cabin. Ghana Airways displayed such a model in its London offices.

Currently, Charlie, Bravo, Bravo Delta and Atlantic Models all supply wooden VC10 models with livery to customer choice. Heathrow Models and Skyline Models were 1/200-scale models sold near London Heathrow Airport. The moulds were reputedly acquired by SMTS Models who in 2016 released several VC10 models with some additional details. Like several larger-scale models, the well-known Aviation Retail Direct are the people to go to secure these and other models of this display type. ADI also market the range of 'Sky Classics' VC10 models.

Manufacturer British Classic Aircraft offered a 1/100 VC10 up to 2011 via the Collectors Aircraft Models shop (CAM) several years ago.

Decals for many VC10 liveries can be found via TwoSix Decals, RAM Models and F-DCAL. All decals are for 1/144-scale models – ideal for Airfix and Roden kits.

Below: The East African Super VC10 was the ultimate version of the airframe with all the enhancements and improvements learned during the VC10 design process. The EAA Super VC10s were owned by the three East African countries that formed EAA and the flags on the tailfin represented each nation according to the aircraft's registration. The interiors were as brightly coloured as the exteriors.

Bottom: The hybrid mid-1970s scheme of the BOAC-to-British Airways merger led to a mixed livery for over a year.

The full, new BA livery as the Negus scheme looked smart on the VC10 but many lamented the loss of the Speedbird emblem on the tailfin. The emblem was designed in the 1930s. This is the Sky Classics moulding.

Classic VC10 colours seen in BA and BUA at 1/400 by Gemini and Jet-X, respectively.

The final RAF VC10 era was celebrated with three special tailfin liveries applied to VC10s. Gemini modelled them and here we see two side by side displaying the superb detailing and direct printing achieved despite the 1/500-scale limitations.

AIRFIX 1/144

Airfix made a well-detailed injection-moulded VC10 but like many VC10 kits, it curiously lacked the vital tall inboard wing fences of the real airframe. Modellers would have to retrofit these for accuracy. But the Airfix kit was the pioneer and very accurate in details from fin to dihedral and contours. Only the engine mounting angle seemed to be of minor concern – with the engines at the original angle not the revised angle as applied by Vickers to later airframes.

With a little bit of filler work, and the use of plastic sheet to create the inboard wing fence, the Airfix kit was of sufficient quality to create a professional standard kit.

Originally marketed in the earlier BOAC blue and white livery with two white bands and white Speedbird emblem on the fin, then in British Airways colours and finally as an RAF K2 tanker machine, this kit provided the mainstay of the VC10 kit enthusiast for many years. First issued in late 1964, and reissued as late as 2003 (model number 04026), the Airfix kit lent itself to accurate modelling and

expert-standard modification. The modeller could create a fleet of VC10s using decal kits of other airlines. Modification to Super VC10 dimensions was also easily possible. A recent decal set from TwoSix Decals and a degree of modification can turn an Airfix tanker into an early BOAC Standard livery.

Building the Airfix VC10 Kit

As the accompanying photographs depict, the basic kit can offer a true rendition; however, extra work with trimming, fillers, re-contouring can add vital forensic accuracy to the VC10/Super VC10 kit build. Of note, the VC10 modeller can address any nose contour moulding issues, extend the fuselage, reconfigure the engine mountings angle for Super VC10 types, and refine the wing leading edges and wingtips for the Standard Type 1102 and 1103 VC10 variants.

Adding the inboard wing fence across all kits is an obvious must. Numerous liveries are available from decal suppliers – even the Nigeria Airways schemes. A rarity to create would be the Air Malawi VC10 7Q-QYKH.

This view of a very rare 1960s-era issue Airfix VC10 has been built by Gert Meijer and displays the very early BOAC VC10 livery with the white Speedbird emblem and two white horizontal tailfin lines – as seen on the early 1963–1964 VC10s and the initial Airfix box art and decal set.

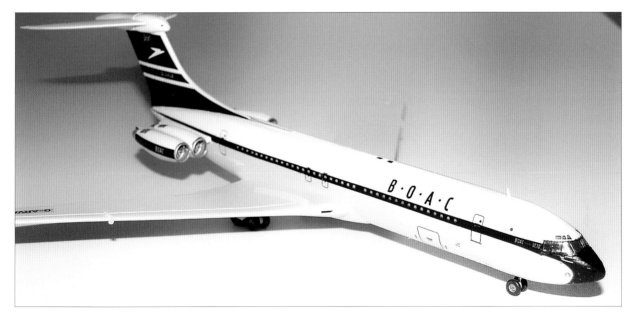

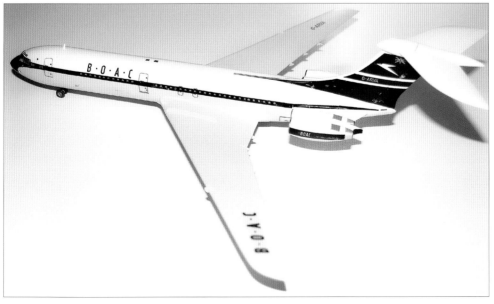

As can be seen in this rare model, Gert has captured the early specification with four thrust reversers. He has also added the vital in-board wing fences that were missing from the Airfix tooling. Key details like aerials, pitot tubes and door mouldings can all be seen.

Expert modeller, Australian David Connolly (Skypirate on the unoffical Airfix Modelling forum), put a massive amount of work into converting the Airfix tanker moulding into the defining RAF all-white VC10 classic. Attention to the engine stub wings, wing fences, and fuselage and window details have all produced a defining RAF VC10 tribute that really does capture the essence of the VC10.

Above: David says of the model: "This model was the later Airfix tanker version, backdated to the transport C.1, since the airliner version was no longer generally available."

The exquisite level of detail seen here in David's Airfix conversion includes the cargo door, engine pod detail and variable incidence tailplane. This is top-level modelling that closely matches the full-scale original.

Paul Janicki built this superb Airfix kit with expert-level modifications to all the relevant moulding and technical points. He used recently produced decals from 26 Decals and fine-tuned the moulding and its appearance to make a wonderful tribute to Air Malawi's 7Q-YKH on which he had flown many years ago. This is the Airfix kit taken to the best level.

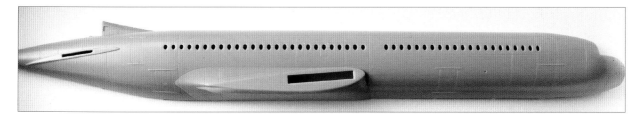

RODEN 1/144

In 2015, Ukraine-based Roden produced and issued two 1/144-scale Super VC10 kits and these quickly sold out. The kits contained decals for EAA 5H-MMT and BOAC G-ASGI respectively. The kit as a new release includes good detailing. Clearly similarly to the old Airfix and Frog toolings, it is interesting that the kits also offer RAF tanker variant components which allow building a K3 or K4 tanker version. In May 2016, Roden VC10 code-327 was announced which created the build K3 ZA149. In February 2017, kit code-328 was released. This kit includes decals to create K4 ZD241 as seen preserved at Bruntingthorpe airfield.

The Roden kit was finely detailed and even showed the one-piece window reinforcing plates of the real airframe. Wing plating and even details such as door frames and reinforcements were all accurately portrayed. Filler work was required over the upper nose fuselage components however. The kit came with good decals, and a rather nice illustration card.

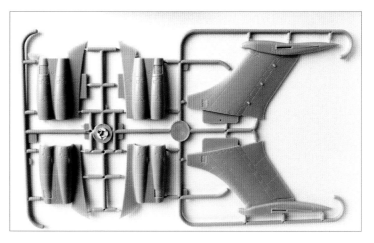

Roden's moulding was seemingly of slightly lighter gauge than the original Airfix moulding, yet well marked and shaped. However some work is required to remove the parts from the sprue and create a finer finish. The engine pods and thrust-reverser details were well executed. Some internal bracing of the fuselage might be advisable. Only the cutaway nose and cockpit moulding seems an anomaly.

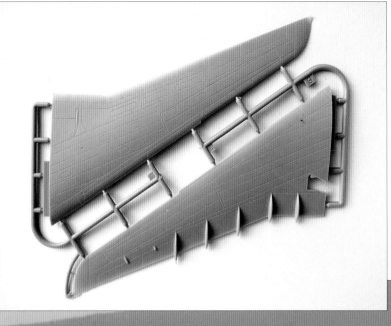

Although accurate and well detailed, the Roden wingtips are thin. They, and the leading edges, require some work with a knife and the filler pack. The inboard wing fence is offered, but could be taller to be more accurate in scale.

Up close the model reveals good scaling, correct dimensions and accurate panel work; however, quite a bit of remedial and modification work is required to the basic Roden moulding. In this model built by Ian Woodward in BOAC Speedbrid colours, the sheer level of expertise required to meet the highest modelling standards is revealed – as seen at the Britmodeller website where VC10 enthusiasts gather.

Another angle on Ian Woodward's excellent Roden Super VC10 build displays the correct shapes and scales to features such as the engines, fin top bullet fairing and the difficult-to-render nose and cockpit details, including the pitot fitting and windscreens.

WELSH MODELS 1/144

Vac-formed and metal part kits: Model VC10 K3/K4 Tanker (2006 release). EAA decals 2006 and BOAC kit and decal releases 2007. Scale 1/144. An interesting vac-formed and metal accessory part hybrid kit. It seems Welsh Models produced both the Standard and Super VC10 as kits in their respective dimensions and offered airline and RAF decals. Interestingly, decal kits for the BOAC version show registrations G-ARVB and G-ASGA, as Standard and Super VC10s respectively. Post-2006, the RAF tanker versions were still available and are now obvious on the second-hand market. From 2007, a BOAC kit and then EAA decals have been cited with Welsh Models. An interesting and rewarding project for the VC10 kit-builder enthusiast.

RAM MODELS 1/72

This post-2015 kit was a rare vac-formed 1/72 scale kit and was depicted as an RAF C.Mk.1 and, although web-referenced, now appears to be no longer available. RAM used the prior Airways vac form tooling. Still a current kit with livery and type options available. Ideal for custom-building of a special VC10 type.

FROG, NOVO 1/144

This now rare, early 1970s kit has long been out of production but at its launch with the BOAC VC10 in service, it was an interesting kit as it included working flashing navigation lights. Batteries to power the lighting were fitted by an under-fuselage hatch. This kit was at 1/144 scale with injection-moulded parts and BOAC decals for Super VC10 G-ASGD, G-ASGF and the marketing-based, non-issued G-BOAC (this registration was later used by a BA Concorde). The Frog kit moulding was later reissued by Novo but without the flashing lights fitted.

This superb build of the Roden Super VC10 in the rare and short-lived BOAC/Cunard livery is by David Griffiths and used 26 Decals, and window decals from Authentic Airliners. David achieved a very accurate SVC10 with attention paid to details such as the aerials and black square housings on the fuselage roof, the wing contours and, of note, the engine intakes. Many hours' work created such a super level of VC10 tribute.

The very rare late 1960s Frog model of the BOAC Super VC10 (as G-BOAC – a fictional registration but one later recreated for Concorde) also featured flashing navigation lights. Its moulding was later reissued by Novo company without the lighting function.

MAGNA MODELS 1/72 VC10

This resin-type kit (MAG9072) builds a 1/72-scaled VC10 C.Mk.1K with decals for the RAF C.Mk.1 XV103 *Edward Mannock VC*. The kit was first released in 2007 and quickly sold out: it is currently listed on many websites as still available. This is a resin kit which includes some white metal parts as detail fittings and requires strong modelling skills to make the most of it.

ANIGRAND 1/72 VC10

Anigrand's resin kit (AA-2096) VC10 K2 tanker ZA141 was of good quality, yet modellers' reviews of the kit's accuracy are variable.

MACH 2 1/72

In 2019 French kit producer Mach 2 released a VC10 kit in three different versions. This is an injection-moulded kit, which is a first for this larger scale. Referenced as GP106–VC10 K2 Camouflaged, GP107–VC10 K2 Low-vis grey, and GP108–Standard VC10 BOAC. Reportedly available in 2020.

GEMINI JETS 1/400

Gems by name and nature, these 1/400-scale metal VC10 renditions are deservedly popular and well detailed. Only some slight heaviness around the wing-fuselage casting detracts from some very accurate casting and colouring in a range of liveries and schemes. Aerials, wheels and logos are all very accurate despite the smaller scale. Gemini has produced over 20 VC10/Super VC10 models in nearly all the liveries – notably that of Middle East Airlines. For the VC10 collector, these models may be small, but they are superb. In 2015, Gemini issued a 1/200 scale VC10 C.Mk.1 as XR808 in the anniversary colour scheme as a one-off issue. Good though it was, it reputedly included an erroneous centreline HDU refuelling hose drum that was not originally fitted to the type.

The Gemini moulding of the engines and their mountings are seen here in this view of the classic BOAC Standard VC10 G-ARVF. The engine pods seem a touch over-scale – more like Conway 550s off a Super VC10 with a differing stub wing and nacelle angle.

It seems that at 1/400 Jet-X and Gemini Jets were in competition to see who could produce the most VC10 and Super VC10 models from their moulds. Gemini's lovely metal models, with direct printing and super detailing, really have become collectors' items. Only the wing-to-fuselage joint really gives the game away. One notable point is that the Gemini models of the Standard VC10 seem to lack its nose-down stance. This is less obvious in the Super VC10 as it lost most of that stance due to the longer forward fuselage.

Above: Time-warp time: Gemini's BOAC and Nigeria Airways machines in contemporary 1960s colours show off just how different the VC10 could look dependent on colour schemes. Both these models depict the two outboard-thrust reverser-only configuration latterly applied to the VC10 and all but very early, Super VC10s. Tailplane buffet and fatigue was reduced by deleting the in-board reversers.

Centre left: The Standard VC10 had just one (little used) rear side door (on the right side), whereas the Super VC10 had rear doors on both sides; the left-side door was used as a passenger-loading door. The Gemini wing fence and engines are seen detailed here.

Bottom left: Engine details seen up close. Even at this scale, the fuel-dump rods on the outboard flap 'canoe' fairing are moulded.

Facing page top: Nigeria Airways 5N-ABD was often seen parked next to a BOAC Standard at London Heathrow, so why not as models? Gemini aircraft had movable tailplanes – great care was needed to avoid issues.

Facing page middle: Not unlike the MEA VC10 livery, this early Nigeria Airways scheme was soon modernized as can be seen in the Sky Classics Nigeria Airways model shots included herein.

Facing page bottom: Super detailing at 1/400 scale shows off the vital details on the forward fuselage.

Three VC10s of the Gemini range displaying the differences in design and markings. The RAF 'red tail' 40th Anniversary machine even has its electronics aerials modelled. A fine achievement at this scale from Gemini.

VC10/Super VC10 in resin/plastic/vac kit scale models
Roden 1/144
Mach 2 1/72
Airfix 1/144
Frog 1/144
Welsh Models 1/144
Airways Vac Form /RAM Models 1/72
Magna Models 1/72
Anigrand 1/72
Westaway 1/24

Metal scale models
Heathrow Models
British Classic Aircraft
Skyline Models
Sky Classics
Aero Mini
Gemini Jets
Corgi Aviation Archive
Inflight 500
AeroClassics
JetX
JC Wings
First Choice
Herpa

Desktop models/wooden/hybrid
Charlie Bravo Models
Bravo Delta Models
Atlantic Models
Nice Airplanes
Planecraft

Seen from underneath, the Jet-X Ghana VC10 did not disappoint – given the small scale. The undercarriage was harder to render at this scale, of course. Jet-X were not the first to try a 1/400 scale VC10 in metal – Aeroclassics produced a model in 1998. It used decals rather than printing for the markings.

The later British United Airways (BUA) colours seen on a Standard VC10 model (left) and as the same aircraft's later post-British Caldenonian1974 reconfiguration as the Sultan of Oman Royal Flight VC10 in its unique livery (the actual airframe is now resident at Brooklands Museum Trust). Both liveries were part of more than 20 VC10 colour schemes available from Gemini.

BOAC VC10/Super VC10 multi-scale collection depicting the key liveries used by the airline between 1963 and 1974 prior to its merger with BEA, to form British Airways. Note the differing wing mouldings and treatments as well as the livery cheatline differences.

After BOAC and BEA merged, BOAC's VC10 fleet flew in a hybrid ex-BOAC colour scheme featuring the new BA tailfin colours (known as the Negus scheme), but with the old BOAC cheatline in blue. It took several years for the VC10 and Super VC10 fleets to be fully repainted.

Left: G-ASIX in the final BUA scheme at 1/400 scale. Only the engine pods seem out of scale, being a touch too large.

Below: The stunning East African Airways multinational tri-nation colours depicted on the Super VC10 in the Gemini range. Despite the small scale, the detailing is superb, although the wing-fuselage join is inevitably slightly coarse. A much-sought-after model on the second-hand market.

Corgi's wonderful 1/144 renditon of the first BOAC Standard VC10 in the early BOAC colours with gold edging to the cheatline and two white stripes on the fin. This second Corgi release dealt with the previous cockpit moulding-line issue. A rare model indeed and a true classic.

Stemming from the early 2000s, the attractive Ghana Airways later livery (version 2) was portrayed on the Jet-X brand 1/400 model, which remains available from airline model specialists. Jet-X produced the Ghana Airways VC10s 9G-ABO and G-ABP with varying logo types. Of note, Jet-X produced a BOAC/BA 1974–1975-era BOAC-BA hybrid livery that depicted the changeover colour scheme prior to full BA colours on the VC10 fleet. Rarest of all the Jet-X VC10 models was A40-AB of 2007, the Omani livery.

Seen in the most famous Ghana Airways livery, the Jet-X metal model of the Standard VC10 was well executed. The differing colours were correctly captured as were many of the airframe details and features. The tailfin logo was a key element in the Ghana colours. Jet-X have made 20 types of VC10 model liveries.

Available from Aviation Retail Direct (ARD); at its shop near London Heathrow it offers possibly the widest range of VC10 models currently available: the 1/200-scale Sky Classics range of VC10/Super models (which appear to make use of an earlier mould) are well known. Despite a couple of issues with some contours and certain livery details, these are popular models that have rendered the look of the VC10 well across a range of civil liveries and military markings.

Seen here is the second (later) Nigeria Airways livery, which was bolder than its simpler forebear. In this Sky Classics model (SC304) at the Sky Classics 1/200 scale, the essence of the green and white VC10 is obvious. The tailfin angle and tailplane sweep are correctly rendered.

VC10 tailpiece. Looking as a VC10 should, this is a great angle from which to see the VC10. That the VC10 would continue to serve from 2006 to 2013, seems a fitting tribute to a machine that entered RAF service in 1966 (and airline service in 1964).

Sky Classics have produced the RAF VC10/Squadron 40th Anniversary markings (red tail) and 90th Anniversary'(black tail) very effectively. The printing is of high quality, although some enthusiasts find some of the airframe details a little prominent. Note the underwing refuelling pods.

Sky Classic also make the RAF 101 Squadron Super VC10 tanker conversion in its later markings. Seen here with the RAF C.Mk.1 in the background, this Super VC10 K.Mk.3 depicts ZA149 – the ex-EAA 5XUVJ – as seen with rear under-fuselage unit fitted.

Sky Classics have also produced the quintessential white and blue Royal Air Force C.Mk.1 VC10 with cargo door as XV102, in all its classic glory. This really looks the part.

The same aircraft seen from the front with the refuelling probe in situ.

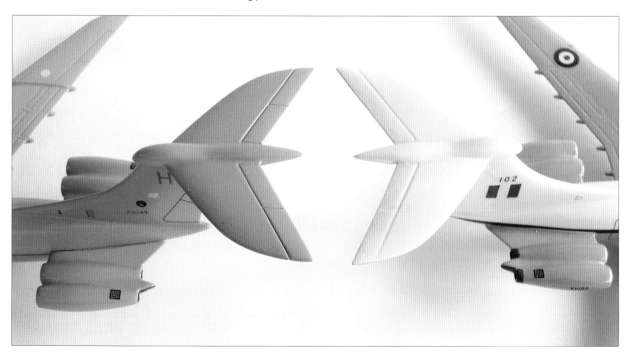

ZA 149 and XV102 Sky Classics livery differences as captured in a tail study that shows off the correct shape of the fin-top bullet fairing and airframe.

RAF classics. Several decades and thousands of flying hours separated the white RAF VC10 C.Mk.1 story and the later matt grey K.Mk.3 and K.Mk.4 operations. The subtle differences in wing design and fuselage specification are seen here in the Sky Classics collection.

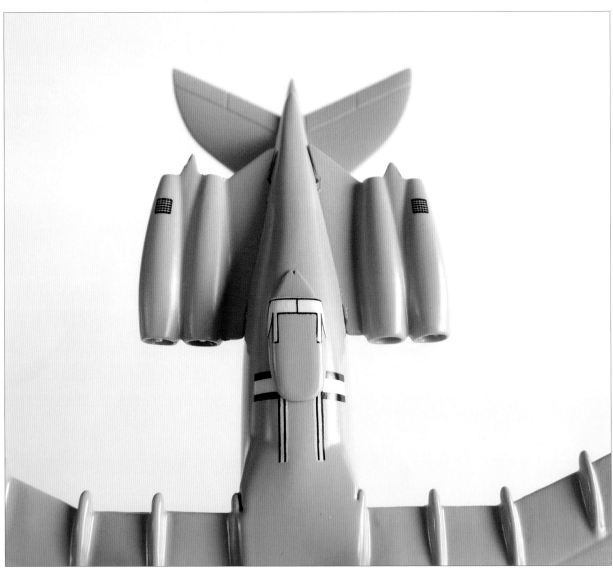

Refuelling HDU and engine stub wing details as well as flap fairings are seen in the underbody view of the K.Mk.4 model.

Above: In this view of the Sky Classics Anniversary VC10 C.Mk.1model of XV105 as it was re-engineered into C.Mk.1K, the model's engine pods, main wing/airframe details, including the, fence, spoilers and flap panels are all detailed. The fin is correctly depicted.

Centre: XV 104 the C.Mk.1 converted to C.Mk.1K seen in the superb 40th Anniversary colours as available in the Sky Classics range. Only some minor issues with the nose contours are likely to be noted by VC10 enthusiasts in this series – as can be seen from this angle.

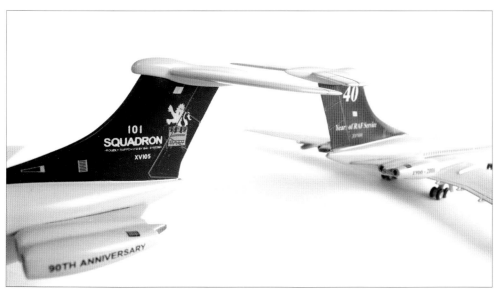

Left: Essential VC10 details of design – two tails showing off the lines that made the aircraft, and today's models, so popular. It is vital to get the tailfin, fairing and tailplanes correct in any model – be it kit or die-cast or plastic or wooden moulding. Note engine beaver tail exhausts The printing details of the livery are also critical ingredients.

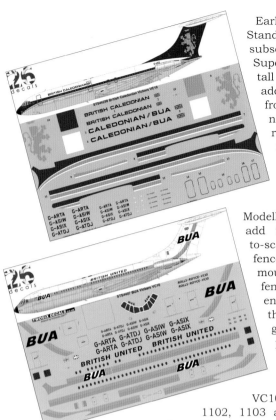

26 Decals have produced a series of superb decal kits for the VC10, including the British United Airways livery schemes and British Caledonian VC10 decal set – as depicted here in the laser-like detail.

Early Type 1001 BOAC Standard VC10s, all subsequent VC10s and Super VC10s had the tall in-board wing fence added. This was missing from the Airfix kit, but not the Roden kit. Airfix rushed their kit out for 1965 and modelled it on the prototype VC10 drawings and images (G-ARTA being the subject). Modellers need to build and add their own accurate-to-scale in-board wing fences. On the Roden moulding of this wing fence, it is neither tall enough to scale, nor thin enough. Time to get the thin-gauge plastic modelling card out and the filler and make your own.

Post-Type 1101 VC10s such as the Types 1102, 1103 and RAF Types, and Super VC10s, all lost the full chord outer wing fence that the BOAC Type 1101 had featured. Instead, these types featured a leading-edge-only mini-fence at the same span position. Later Types 1102, 1103, RAF and Supers, also gained the small, stepped 4 percent chord extension visible at the leading edge.

Other key factors include changes to inspection plates on the upper and lower wing surfaces, changes to the wing root inlet opening for the air-conditioning unit, and other changes to local panel work.

The VC10 series also saw at least three types of engine/exhaust nacelle tail shapes applied as the so-called beaver tail exhausts and the modeller can consult period photographs for accurate reference points on these.

Variations in aerials, electronics fitments and tyres, all need to be considered when modelling the VC10 across its variants. Latterly, all RAF VC10s received window

-edge reinforcement lips, and the tanker fleet of course saw many windows deleted.

Some modellers prefer to fill in all the windows on civil or military models, delete the clear plastic model kit windows as supplied, and rely upon printed window decals. This is a matter of personal choice. So too is weathering. Some modellers feel that adding engine, exhaust and reverse-thrust soot to the VC10 kit is worthwhile. Others disagree.

Often missing from VC10 models is the 10-degree main undercarriage rake and the slight nose-down pitch of the fuselage as seen on the ground.

Given the errors in moulding of commercial kits concerning the VC10 and Super VC10 engine stub wings in dimensions and angles of set, it is interesting to note that some moulded engine and stub wing kits are available – notably from Braz models.

Recent VC10 livery decals from 26 Decals and other suppliers have allowed great scope for adding laser-printed liveries and effects. Other VC10 accessories have come from RAM and Braz. Kits from Airfix, Roden and others all require fine tuning, trimming, filling and work on some panel lines, hatches and mouldings. It is these factors that take the VC10 modeller into the realms of expertise and realism.

Another area of note are the nose contours and cockpit/flight deck windows. Also crucial to the correct modelling of the VC10 family is an accurate rendition of the fin-top bullet fairing.

Modellers are therefore aware of the many differences in wing shapes that the VC10 can be built with. Might the ultimate remaining build be a VC10 with the single Rolls-Royce RB211 engine test bed mounted on the port side and relevant markings on the ex-RAF airframe?

The aircraft remains a firm favourite with modellers and has many options to explore. All these years on, the VC10, like other famous airframe icons, is seeing new models and new decals being produced for the market, and proves that demand and interest are strong for this amazing aeroplane.

Acknowledgements
Jelle Hieminga and VC10.net, Paul Burge at Aviation Retail Direct, Ray Charles at 26 Decals, Britmodeller, Paul Janicki, The Unoffical Airfix Modellers Forum, Skypirate David Connolly, Gert Meijer, David Griffiths, Brooklands Museum Trust and Julian Temple at Brooklands Museum, Duxford Aviation Society, British Airways historical archive, Christopher Orlebar, Brian Trubshaw, Sir George Edwards, Brooklands ex-Vickers staff and volunteers, Julian Temple and Brooklands VC10 anniversary materials. Further sources include *Vickers VC10*, Lance Cole (Crowood Press), *VC10: Icon of the Skies*, Lance Cole (Pen & Sword Books) and references therefrom, 'VC10: A

Niche in History', J.R. Finnimore, Putnam Aeronautical Review, BOAC and BA press material, *The Aeroplane, Flight International* and archive, Royal Air Force Brize Norton. Luchtvaarthobbyshop and Froude & Hext Models, with thanks to Bob and Chris. Photographs are by the author or sourced from BOAC/BA press material, and Vickers BAC archives at Brooklands Museum Trust. Thanks and acknowledgements to the above and all who have helped. All efforts have been made to ascertain photographic credits where possible. (Note: Lance F. Cole as author, has no connection to the UK photographic online website cited as Lance Cole Photography or its works or actions.)